The Green Library Planner

What Every Librarian Needs to Know Before Starting to Build or Renovate

Mary M. Carr

THE SCARECROW PRESS, INC.
Lanham • Toronto • Plymouth, UK
2013

Published by Scarecrow Press, Inc.
A wholly owned subsidiary of The Rowman & Littlefield Publishing Group, Inc.
4501 Forbes Boulevard, Suite 200, Lanham, Maryland 20706
www.rowman.com

10 Thornbury Road, Plymouth PL6 7PP, United Kingdom

British Library Cataloguing in Publication Information Available

Library of Congress Cataloging-in-Publication Data

Carr, Mary M., 1950–
The green library planner : what every librarian needs to know before starting to build or renovate /
Mary M. Carr.
p. cm.
Includes bibliographical references and index.
ISBN 978-0-8108-8736-7 (pbk. : alk. paper) — ISBN 978-0-8108-8737-4 (ebook) 1. Library build-
ings—Environmental aspects. 2. Library buildings—Energy conservation. 3. Library buildings—
Design and construction. 4. Library buildings—Remodeling. 5. Sustainable buildings. I. Title.
Z679.85.C37 2013
022'.3—dc23
2013018124

♾ ™ The paper used in this publication meets the minimum requirements of American
National Standard for Information Sciences Permanence of Paper for Printed Library
Materials, ANSI/NISO Z39.48-1992.

Printed in the United States of America

Contents

Acknowledgments

I would like to dedicate this work to my mother, Annella M. Winkes (1917–2011), and my father, Everett F. Winkes (1911–1991), both children of the Great Depression. Teachers first and always, they taught their children the principles of sustainability and the gentle use of the Earth's resources.

I would also like to extend a heartfelt thank you to both Brenda Martinson and Dr. Julie B. Todaro for reading the manuscript, carefully proofreading it, and offering helpful suggestions. Your support is greatly appreciated. I owe you one. Well, actually, I owe you both more than that!

Introduction

Creativity is piercing the mundane to find the marvelous.—Bill Moyers

IMAGINING SUSTAINABILITY

As stated in the American Library Association's Libraries Build Sustainable Communities webpage, "In one way or another, everyone is connected as part of a living system."[1] And, one way or the other, the buildings we inhabit are also a part of that same living system.

If you are reading this book, you are probably one of many types of stakeholders involved in building or renovating a library. You are probably also very aware that the decisions you make today regarding your library will affect your community for years to come. Sustainability is about thinking through all the ways that this might happen and addressing as many of them as you can.

Look around your community. Imagine what life in that community will be like one hundred years from now. What do you see? What needs will your community have? What will your library look like? How will it reflect the community it serves? How will it become a community center? How gentle will it be on the environment, both in the way it is built and the way it operates? What sustainable qualities will draw the community to it? What sustainable community qualities will the building reflect? In essence, what decisions can you make now regarding your library to ensure that your community will be worth working, living, and learning in by 2100?

As the ALA website suggests, sustainable community development is "a process for making choices about the future." It is about considering the three basic elements of your community—its economy, environment, and social equity—as you chart a course that will take your library and community toward a sustainable future. Everyone involved in your building, from the design team to the library staff to the public, needs to imagine how your library might contribute to the practice of sustainable development in your community. Can your building be a model for other development projects? Can your library host a sustainability center? Can your library house a collection of sustainability resources? Can you offer sustainability programming? What else might you imagine? What can you create?

The greatest challenge for teams working on sustainable or green development is imagination: thinking outside the box instead of doing things the time-tested way. Thinking creatively means considering all the ways that your building can affect the world around it—and finding all the solutions to challenges that might arise. A good way to jumpstart your imagination is to look at what other cutting-edge developers have done. The Green Libraries website[2] is the most comprehensive list of green library buildings available on the web and offers fascinating examples.

Look also at some of the imaginative libraries that have been built recently in Europe, like The Hive in Worcestershire, England.[3] The Hive is a joint public and university library—the first of its kind in Europe. It is home to the county's Archives and Archaeology Service, one of the largest children's libraries in the United Kingdom, a contemporary business center with meeting rooms and a conference facility, and a customer contact center (the first point of contact for the local county and district councils).

The Hive is designed to be modern and cutting edge, embracing new, ecofriendly technology. For example, this iconic new building draws water from the River Severn as part of its high-tech, ecofriendly ventilation system. The Hive is a building that "responds to its brief and setting, and uses sustainable materials that will endure. It is accessible by all people, provides a safe environment and is welcoming to anyone who comes through the doors. To help users identify where they feel most comfortable, each area within The Hive is defined by colour, lighting and acoustics to create distinct and appropriate zones."[4] The project has won several awards for its innovative and sustainable design, including the 2012 Partnerships Award for the Best Sustainability in a Project.

Another project of note is the Mountain of Books Library Quarter,[5] which is part of a larger plan to breathe new life into the town of Spijkenisse, located within the Rotterdam metropolitan area. A series of commercial and community spaces are stacked into a pyramid-shaped structure, which is wrapped in a 480-meter-long bookcase. The glass facades fully expose the library shelves, inviting people to step in and grab a book. Most importantly, the architecture was conceived as a way to address the community's 10 percent illiteracy rate. Hoping to intrigue and instill interest, the library was designed as a huge advertisement for reading and placed it at the heart of the development. The shape of the building alludes to traditional Dutch farms, a reminder of the town's agricultural past. In addition to the library,

> the building houses an environmental education center, a chess club area, auditoriums, meeting rooms, commercial offices, and retail space. A café at the top of the pyramid offers panoramic views of the town.
>
> Another reference to rural life resides in the bookshelf design, made of recycled flowerpots. Fireproof and economic, the versatile shelves accompany visitors throughout the building, merging with banisters, parapets, and the information desk.
>
> The library has no air conditioning, relying instead on natural ventilation and sun screens to ensure a comfortable indoor climate. In winter, an innovative combination of underground heat storage, floor heating, and double glazing keeps the building warm.
>
> To visually connect the new structure to the existing townscape, the architects used a brick wall—a ubiquitous material in the local architecture—to separate the library from the rest of the building. This created a brick core visible through the glass walls.
>
> The same material was used in the treatment of the surrounding piazza and in the residential buildings in the Library Quarter, creating a unifying image for the whole ensemble that further emphasizes the luring glow of the Book Mountain.[6]

The people in Worcestershire and Spijkenisse who designed these buildings are no more imaginative than you, your design team, your library staff, and your community. Be inspired by their accomplishments and set out to renovate or build a library as inspirational, imaginative, and befitting of your community.

And, lastly, to stir your imagination as you begin this think about and design your new library building or renovation, take a look at *58 Novel Library Designs.*[7] Be amazed by the clever, adaptive re-use and recycling ideas. What possibilities exist for your project? What works in your library and with your community? What can you and your community imagine?

BUILDING VS. RENOVATION

Sustainability is easiest to achieve when starting with a brand-new building. But those seeking to remodel will find the information contained in this work useful as well. Depending on the extent of the remodel, it may not be possible to approach a remodeling project in an integrated manner, one of the cornerstones of green building. For instance, if you need to replace a furnace, it is certainly important to purchase one that is energy efficient and has an Energy Star rating. However, if your library building is not sufficiently insulated, or your windows leak or your building faces north and is swept by a cold wind, your library will not receive the benefit it might from that furnace, unless all the building envelope factors were addressed or mitigated.

Nonetheless, there is lots you can do in a piecemeal manner. Perhaps you can plan for a renovation, but approach it bit by bit, as funding allows. If this is your situation, it's best to come up with an integration plan and treat the project like a phased renovation, rather than as a piecemeal remodel.

YOUR SUSTAINABLE LIBRARY

In the past two decades, enthusiasts have turned the green building phenomenon to a major part of the design and construction industry. Leadership in Energy and Environmental Design (LEED®),[8] an internationally recognized suite of rating systems from the U.S. Green Building Council (USGBC), can be used a barometer for this transformation. At last count, the USGBC reported over 9 billion square feet of building space participating in the LEED suite of rating systems, with 1.6 million feet certifying per day around the world.[9] According to the USGBC, the Green Building Certification Institute now accepts more applications to certify renovations than to certify new buildings.[10] Meanwhile, during these last two decades, many more buildings have been built or renovated using green features without seeking LEED or any other certification. Clearly green building has moved into the mainstream.

Because green building is here to stay, there is need for an accessible work covering the major aspects of green building as it applies to building libraries, renovating them, and operating them sustainably. This volume is intended to fill that need. It presents an overall philosophy of sustainability and the basic concepts and terminology used to design, construct, and operate green libraries based on state-of-the-art design and construction practices in 2013. It is written for a wide array of possible readers: librarians who need an introduction to the rationale for green buildings, the elements of green building, and the language of the field; public officials, boards, or administrators who are considering a new green library building, a renovated library structure, or sustainable elements for a current library facility; residents interested in approaching the design, construction, and operation of community facilities in a more responsible and sustainable way; and of course professionals and designers working on sustainable projects.

The *Planner*'s foundation will be the elements of green building, despite the type of structure, but it will also include elements particular to libraries, what they represent, and what they need. The information included here is technically accurate and up-to-date, but you won't need a professional or technical background to understand the concepts. Moreover, it is a planner that will assist you in transforming your library into a building that treats the environment gently and provides your community with a model and the knowledge of how to do so.

The chapters that follow will address the fundamental concepts and essential elements of green building. Chapter 1 covers the basic tenets of green building. The following chapters address specific topics: place (chapter 2), energy and lighting (chapter 3), green materials (chapter 4), air quality (chapter 5), water use (chapter 6), construction management (chapter 7), and finally operations and maintenance (chapter 8).

With this information the librarian, related library staff, administrators, board members, library patrons, and the library's partners will be able to build and operate the library in the best way to address the environmental and economic challenges of the twenty-first century. What are the important new sustainable technologies that are influencing the building industry? What programs and services, both now and envisioned, will occupy the spaces? What partnerships might be possible to promote in this green endeavor? What can I do in my library, in my educational setting, or in my city or county to further the green building revolution?

GREEN RESOURCES AND GREEN CREDENTIALS

Throughout the text I rely on my own experience and on published data current through 2013. Most of these data are available from the U.S. Green Building Council, published works, Internet sources, and business or trade media. The resources I have used are reflected in the footnotes and the Resources list at the end of each chapter.

I have been a librarian since 1973, a sustainable building advisor since 2008, and a LEED AP since 2009. I have taught green sustainable building, am a frequent speaker at conferences and workshops, and have applied the concepts, for instance, while helping to write the City of Spokane's Sustainability Plan and while serving as a member of Spokane's Main Market Co-op Board of Directors. I am now in my second term as a member of the ACRL/ LLAMA Interdivisional Committee on Building Resources. What I know now I wish I had known back in the 1980s, when I was first involved in building a new library. But that's the nature of experience and of a green building movement that came into its own in the decades that followed.

What I know now, however, can benefit you, the reader. I see my role as a bridge between green building professionals and the larger library community. Using this *Green Library Planner*, librarians can improve their understanding of the importance of green library buildings and the process used to ensure that the project results in the greenest building possible. Green buildings are better buildings. In fact, buildings use 36 percent of the energy in the United States, according to the U.S. Environmental Protection Agency.

Buildings that use less energy help to address the very real challenges of peak oil and climate change. They also provide indoor environments and outside aesthetics that are more hospitable to the occupants.[11]

As centers for learning, libraries should be places where people can learn more about sustainability, both the philosophy and its practices. The library world has an important role to play in transforming library buildings into ones that represent what people say they want: energy- and resource-efficient, environmentally sound, healthy, comfortable, and productive places to live, work, learn, and recreate. As teaching and learning centers, libraries also set examples from which the communities they serve can learn. Library staff can use the building itself as a teaching tool, implementing unique educational programs addressing the building's green features. These programs can take the form of exhibits or special programs, and a collection of green building and sustainability materials can be developed to complement the green building and its green programming.

At the end of each chapter, I have included two special sections: Examples and Your Project Notes. The first section provides examples of well-built, green libraries that embody the concepts outlined in that chapter. The Project Notes section offers questions that may be useful to address in order to thoroughly consider your own library project. I have also left room for your notes and questions related to your project.

I hope this *Green Planner* will help you understand the importance of green building and the critical need for you to be knowledgeable and a fully participating building design team member. You are every bit as important as the contractor, if you are to have a building that functions in the best way possible for the employees, the patron, and the larger community it serves.

Thank you for your interest in sustainability and green library buildings. May you read this *Green Library Planner* and begin your integrated planning process armed with the information needed to remodel, renovate, or build the best green library building your resources can afford. As Bill Moyers notes in the quote that opens this introduction, we must understand the mundane and embrace it, but then "pierce" it to move beyond and find the "marvelous"— the new and imaginative possibilities that we all have inside us. I hope that this planner helps you find those possibilities.

I welcome any and all feedback. Please direct it to me at mmcspo@yahoo.com.

NOTES

1. "Libraries Build Sustainable Communities," American Library Association, accessed December 2, 2012, http://www.ala.org/srrt/tfoe/lbsc/librariesbuildsustainablecommunitiesintroduction.
2. Monika Antonelli, *Green Libraries: A Website for Information about Green and Sustainable Libraries*, accessed December 2, 2012, http://www.greenlibraries.org/.

3. The Hive, accessed December 2, 2012, http://www.thehiveworcester.org/.

4. The Hive.

5. The Atlantic Cities, accessed December 2, 2012, http://www.theatlanticcities.com/design/2012/10/climb-mountain-books/3513/.

6. *The Atlantic Cities.*

7. "58 Novel Library Designs," Trendhunter, accessed August 27, 2012, http://www.trendhunter.com/slideshow/library-designs.

8. The U.S. Green Building Council policy is to use *LEED*—with the registered trademark superscript—for the first use in a short document, or the first use in each section of a longer document. Following the first mention, the policy is to use *LEED*.

9. "What LEED Is?" U.S. Green Building Council, accessed August 27, 2012, http://www.usgbc.org/DisplayPage.aspx?CMSPageID=1988.

10. Pamela Dittmer McKuen, "Chapter 5 LEED-EB and Green Globes CIEB: Rating Sustainable Reconstruction," Building Design + Construction, accessed August 27, 2012, http://www.bdcnetwork.com/chapter-5-leed-eb-and-green-globes-cieb-rating-sustainable-reconstruction.

11. "Greening EPA, EPA Green Buildings," U.S. Environmental Protection Agency, accessed August 27, 2012, http://www.epa.gov/oaintrnt/projects/.

Chapter One

The Fundamentals of Sustainable Building

Man does not weave this web of life. He is merely a strand of it. Whatever he does to the web, he does to himself.—Chief Seattle, 1854

Chief Seattle's words are as true today as they were in 1854. Judging from the depletion of the world's resources that has occurred since then, it is clear that *humans* have been acting as if we wove the web. As a result the world is facing the effects of peak oil and climate change. The scientific community has long agreed that our dependence on fossil fuels inflicts massive damage on the environment and our health, while warming the globe in the process. Should we continue on this course, experts predict substantially increased transportation costs, decreased industrial production, unemployment, hunger, and social chaos as the supplies of the fuels on which we rely dwindle and eventually disappear.

Pulling back from this bleak future requires us to chart a substantially different course . . . and a sustainable one.

WHAT IS SUSTAINABILITY?

There are many definitions of sustainability. In 1987 the United Nations' World Commission on Environment and Development, known as the Brundtland Commission, defined sustainable development as "development which meets the needs of current generations without compromising the ability of future generations to meet their own needs."[1] The Brundtland Commission was named after Norway's former prime minister Gro Harlem Brundtland,

1

who chaired it. Although this is certainly not the only definition, it is the most popular, or at least the most often quoted.

Another well-known, though less quotable, definition of sustainability is offered by the Environmental Protection Agency (EPA). The EPA answers the question "what is sustainability?" in this way:

> Sustainability is based on a simple principle: Everything that we need for our survival and well-being depends, either directly or indirectly, on our natural environment. Sustainability creates and maintains the conditions under which humans and nature can exist in productive harmony, that permit fulfilling the social, economic and other requirements of present and future generations.[2]

Sustainability is important to making sure that we continue to have the water, materials, and resources to protect human health and our environment. Simply put, a system is sustainable when its operation does not break it down over time—in other words, when resources that are consumed are replenished.[3]

Green is a word that is used interchangeably with *sustainability. Green,* as defined in the *Oxford English Dictionary*, is "pertaining to or supporting environmentalism." The various definitions of sustainability speak to a balance among the planet, the economy, and people. This balance is something that Chief Seattle recognized many years ago. To remember these three elements, the sustainability community uses one of two mnemonics: the *three Es* (economy, environment, and social equity) or the *three Ps* (profit, planet, and people). These elements are also known as the *triple bottom line.* A Venn diagram is often used to illustrate sustainability; figure 1.1 shows the intersection of the three circles in the center of diagram. As illustrated there, the term *green* is actually a narrower term, speaking to the ideals of environmentalism, and does not necessarily encompass the concepts of social equity and economics. That being said, the author, like most others, will sometimes use the term interchangeably.

THE IMPORTANCE OF BUILDINGS IN SUSTAINABILITY EFFORTS

The EPA has defined green building (also known as sustainable or high-performance building) as

> the practice of creating structures and using processes that are environmentally responsible and resource-efficient throughout a building's life cycle from siting to design, construction, operation, maintenance, renovation and deconstruction. This practice expands and complements the classical building design concerns of economy, utility, durability, and comfort.[4]

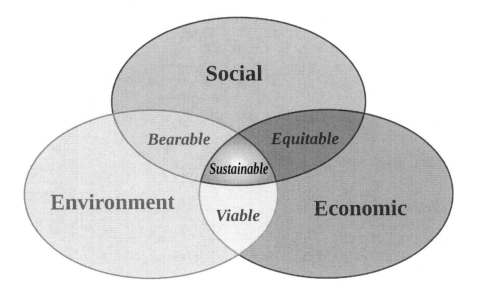

Figure 1.1. Sustainability. Courtesy of Johann Dréo.

Green building practices are a partial answer to the excessive and disproportionate use of the Earth's resources. According to the Worldwatch Institute, the population of the United States represents 5 percent of the world's population, yet its people consume 25 percent of the Earth's fossil fuel resources.[5] If the whole world were to consume resources at that rate, the Earth's population would need the resources of five Earths. Certainly this is anything but sustainable!

Efficient, well-run buildings are an essential part of any effort to move the United States toward a sustainable future because of the considerable amount of energy and resources used in buildings. In fact, according to the U.S. Green Building Council, in the United States buildings alone account for:

- 36 percent of total energy use
- 65 percent of electricity consumption
- 30 percent of greenhouse gas emissions
- 12 percent of potable water
- 30 percent of waste output (136 million tons annually)
- 30 percent of raw materials use[6]

These statistics can be put into perspective when you consider that the transportation sector consumes approximately 28 percent of all end-use energy in the United States.[7] Buildings are a greater "energy suck" than the transportation sector. This is borne out again and again, as is illustrated in an article inelegantly called "Commercial Buildings Are a Huge Energy Suck." The article states that existing commercial buildings in California use over one-third of all the state's energy, but energy-efficient improvements to these commercial buildings could cut those costs by 80 percent. As for new buildings, if requirements were made that tacked on a 2 percent increase in construction costs, new buildings in the Golden State could use one-third to one-half less energy than they use today.[8] California's experience is typical of other places in the United States where green building standards either are lax or do not exist.

WHY BUILD GREEN?

As awareness about the importance of buildings in sustainability efforts has grown, many reports have emerged to support these efforts. These documents are a good place to start understanding the rationale for green building in general and for green libraries in particular:

- The EPA's web page *Why Build Green?* This page addresses the general principles of green building and provides statistics regarding buildings' impact on the environment.[9]
- The Rocky Mountain Institute's report, also called *Why Build Green?* This report lists considerations in green building, provides examples of green construction, and attempts to dispel the notion that green building is more expensive than traditional building processes.[10]
- The American Library Association (ALA) report *Libraries Build Sustainable Communities.* This document addresses specifically green library building. Along with offering concrete suggestions on how libraries can support sustainability efforts, it describes how the "three Es" of sustainability function in relation to libraries: "*Economy* is the management and use of resources to meet household and community needs. *Ecology* is the pattern of relationships between living things and their environment. We all know our shoe size. How many of us know the size of our *ecological footprint*, the amount of air, land and water it takes to support us? *Equity* is fairness. Ideally everyone in a community shares in its well-being. Where there is equity, decisions are based on fairness and *everyone* (regardless of race, income, sex, age, language, sexual orientation, or disability) has opportunities and is treated with dignity."[11] The three Es—economy, ecology, and equity—provide a framework for libraries and their communities to explore. Libraries need to understand all the choices they make today in building and operations and anticipate how those choices, both big and small, will affect tomorrow.

- *Academic Library Building Design: Resources for Planning.*[12] This short online guide provides a starting point for those beginning work on a new building. It lists elements to take into consideration (like use, acoustics, and building regulations like the Americans with Disabilities Act) and provides several lists of resources where stakeholders can find more information on those topics.
- *Sustainable Library Design.*[13] This report is published by Libris Design, the manufacturer of software for library facility-building planning. It introduces readers to the basic concepts and vocabulary of green library building along examples of completed projects.
- The Green Libraries forum on ALA Connect.[14] This forum for members of the American Library Association allows participants to discuss environmental stewardship within our profession and in the communities where we work, live, and play. The topics covered range widely, from solar technologies and greening library programs to academic sustainability curriculum planning.
- IFLA Statement on Libraries and Sustainable Development.[15] This brief text by the International Federation of Library Associations and Institutions states the IFLA's commitment to sustainability in the library field.

These documents are not comprehensive, but they are useful to read because they provide a sense of the public's and library profession's growing commitment to sustainability and provide the philosophical underpinnings of the green building movement.

BASIC PRINCIPLES OF SUSTAINABILITY

As a society, we have grown to understand the importance of preserving our resources for future generations. But when we actually start to plan a building, how do we make decisions that will produce sustainability? Some principles, like using the fewest building materials possible or recycling construction materials, are obvious. But green building depends on several other principles that are just as important.

The Life Cycle

One of the most important tenets of green building is to understand the way your building will continue to affect the environment long after the initial construction is over. A building's existence has an aggregate impact on the environment all the way up and down the supply chain, from *cradle to grave*—the life cycle of the building. A building's costs continue all the while it is in operation, through any renovation or remodeling, through its final demolition. The way to measure this impact is with both life cycle cost analysis and life cycle assessment, each of which tallies the costs of a building from slightly different perspectives and includes slightly different elements.

Life cycle cost analysis (LCCA), according to the Department of Energy, is:

> an economic method of project evaluation in which all costs arising from owning, operating, maintaining, and disposing of a project are considered important to the decision. LCCA is well suited to the economic evaluation of design alternatives that satisfy a required performance level but may have differing investment, operating, maintenance, or repair costs, and possibly different life spans. It is particularly relevant to the evaluation of investments where high initial costs are traded for reduced future cost obligations. [16]

By contrast, EPA defines life cycle assessment (LCA) as:

> a technique to assess the environmental aspects and potential impacts associated with a product, process, or service, by: compiling an inventory of relevant energy and material inputs and environmental releases; evaluating the potential environmental impacts associated with identified inputs and releases; [and] interpreting the results to help you make a more informed decision. [17]

Both methods attempt to more completely determine and express the cost of the building to the owner's pocketbook and, more importantly for the planet, to the environment.

Integrated Design

Another important principle for sustainability is integrated design. This means looking at how each piece of the building's construction and operation will affect all the others. It is a system approach that acknowledges the codependence of all the parts. As in the example given in the introduction, the purchase of an Energy Star furnace is helpful to reducing energy expenditures, but less so if windows leak or insulation is insufficient.

Integrated design is more difficult to achieve when a building is being remodeled rather than built from scratch. But considering carefully the effects of one update on the rest of the building system is still worthwhile.

Integrated Planning

A third principle of sustainable building is iterative, integrated planning. A team representing all the relevant stakeholders for a project should be assembled as early as possible, and these stakeholders should be part of planning every stage of the process, from choosing a site to finishing construction.

Assembling a planning team is discussed in detail in chapter 2, "The Importance of Place," but some basic practices can be outlined here.

One way to achieve integrated planning is the use of charrettes, defined as an "intensive workshop in which various stakeholders and experts are brought together to address a particular design issue," from a single library building to an entire campus or city block. The term can also be applied to "shorter, focused project team meetings, project planning meetings, brainstorming sessions, and extensive community visioning events."[18] Attendance at charrettes by all members is essential for effective planning and communication. Certainly the librarian should be present at each, familiar with the topics under discussion and ready to participate fully, speaking to the library's goals and how these goals will manifest themselves in and fully integrate with the green aspects of the building. In fact the library's goals, should, in part, dictate which of the green options make the most sense to pursue, but the library's goals might also need to be re-imagined in light of green goals.

GREEN BUILDING STANDARDS

The sustainable design movement gained momentum in the 1990s. More and more the question was posed: How do you know if a building is green? The answer came back: develop standards.

Building Research Establishment's Environmental Assessment Method (BREEAM) was the first green building rating system created in the United Kingdom.[19] In 2000, the U.S. Green Building Council (USGBC) followed, developing and releasing criteria also aimed at improving the environmental performance of buildings through its Leadership in Energy and Environmental Design (LEED®) rating system for new construction. Since that first release, LEED has continued to grow in prominence. LEED now includes a number of rating systems for many types of building structures, from existing buildings to hospitals to entire neighborhoods. However, to date, there is no specific standard specifically for library buildings. This planner attempts to bridge that gap by exploring the principles of green building and applying the general principles of green building to the specifics of a library.

Other organizations responded to the growing interest and demand for sustainable design guidelines and standards. The Green Building Initiative (GBI) was created to assist the National Association of Homebuilders (NAHB) in promoting its *Green Building Guidelines for Residential Structures*. Although originally developed for Canada, GBI helped to make Green Globes,[20] the first American National Standards Institute (ANSI) accredited standard, available for use in the United States in 2005. Additional rating systems have been developed that were influenced by these early programs but are tailored to their own national priorities and requirements or seek to go beyond the limits of current policy and building practices to address broader issues of sustainability or evolving concepts such as net zero energy, bio-mimicry, and living and restorative buildings.

While these organizations generally offer certification services, some others simply provide written guidelines for best practices that a building team may choose to follow. For example, the American Society for Heating, Refrigerating and Air Conditioning Engineers (ASHRAE) provides two types of standards for construction of heating, air conditioning, ventilation, and refrigeration systems.[21] The first are consensus documents that reflect minimum standards. The second are advanced design guides that encourage advanced performance. These standards are complex but worth pursuing if a team concludes that they are feasible.

A building team may choose to pursue green certification by an independent certifying organization, but they must also be aware of government guidelines and special programs they may choose to (or have to) follow. Individual states may have their own policies or programs related to public buildings. For example, Washington State was the first state in the union to adopt LEED Silver as a minimum standard for all public buildings larger than 5,000 square feet. Washington State public schools (including their libraries) must also follow the Washington Sustainable Schools Protocol, which is based on the California Collaborative for High Performance Schools.[22] Those sorts of policies are legislated and not optional.

There are also systems that rate individual products used in green library buildings, from equipment to furniture to floor coverings. For instance, Energy Star[23] is a joint program of the U.S. Environmental Protection Agency and the U.S. Department of Energy helping us all save money and protect the environment through certification of energy-efficient products and practices. The Forest Stewardship Council (FSC)[24] certifies wood used throughout the building for furniture, flooring, and many other things as sustainable. The Carpet and Rug Institute's Green Label/Green Label Plus[25] are for flooring, adhesives, and cushions. These examples of the many product standards and guidelines will be included in the chapters that follow, especially chapter 4, "Green Materials."

CONCLUSION

What you do when building or renovating your library building really matters. Your integrated planning and cumulative, accessible, and affordable green choices will result in a building and services that will benefit your bottom line, your community, and the environment. Understanding the philosophy and principles of sustainability will not only help you make effective decisions for your library as you go forward but will allow you to communicate the importance of green library buildings to your community.

YOUR PROJECT NOTES

1. What are the goals of your library's building or renovation project? What do you wish to enhance, improve, or add to your services?

2. How will green library building features aid and enhance the library project goals?

3. What policies and regulations do you need to know as you begin this project? Are you familiar with the green regulations and policies in your city, county, and state?

4. What standards and guidelines would you like to adopt to help meet your library's program goals?

5. What further research for your project must be done before moving on to chapter 2? How might you collect this information in one place, available to everyone on your project design team? Can you use an online tool such as Pinterest?

NOTES

1. UN Economic Commission for Europe, *Sustainable Development: Concept and Action*, http://www.unece.org/oes/nutshell/2004-2005/focus_sustainable_development.html.
2. Environmental Protection Agency (EPA), *Sustainability: What Is Sustainability? What Is EPA Doing? How Can I Help?* http://www.epa.gov/sustainability/basicinfo.htm.
3. "Sustainability," *Eagle Classic Colorado*, http://www.townofeagle.org/index.aspx? NID=254.
4. EPA, *Green Building: Basic Information*, http://www.epa.gov/greenbuilding/pdf/pubs/greenbldg_publist_final.pdf.
5. Worldwatch Institute, *The State of Consumption Today*, http://www.worldwatch.org/node/810.
6. EPA, "Green Buildings: Greening EPA," http://www.epa.gov/oaintrnt/projects/.
7. American Council for an Energy-Efficient Economy, "Transportation Sector: Vehicles and System Efficiency," http://www.aceee.org/portal/transportation.
8. "Commercial Buildings Are an Energy Suck," *The Thin Green Line: An SFGate.com Blog*, July 15, 2010, http://blog.sfgate.com/green/2010/07/15/commercial-buildings-are-a-huge-energy-suck/.
9. EPA, *Green Building: Why Build Green?* http://www.epa.gov/greenbuilding/pubs/whybuild.htm.
10. Alexis Karolides, "Why Build Green?" Rocky Mountain Institute, http://www.rmi.org/Knowledge-Center/Library/D02-14_WhyBuildGreen.
11. "Libraries Build Sustainable Communities," American Library Association, Social Responsibility Round Table (ALA-SRRT) Task Force on the Environment, http://www.ala.org/srrt/tfoe/lbsc/librariesbuild.
12. *Academic Library Building Design: Resources for Planning*, published jointly by the Association of College and Research Libraries (ACRL) and the American Library Association's Library Leadership and Management Association, accessed August 27, 2012, http://wikis.ala.org/acrl/index.php/ACRL/LLAMA_Guide_for_Architects_and_Librarians.
13. Johanna Sands, AIA, *Sustainable Library Design*, published by Libris Design Project, http://www.librisdesign.org/docs/SustainableLibDesign.pdf. The project was supported by the U.S. Institute of Museum and Library Services under the provisions of the Library Services and Technology Act, administered in California by the state librarian.
14. "Green Libraries," ALA Connect, accessed August 27, 2012, http://connect.ala.org/node/71711.
15. "Statement on Libraries and Sustainable Development," IFLA, http://www.ifla.org/en/publications/statement-on-libraries-and-sustainable-development.
16. U.S. Department of Energy, "Guidance on Life-Cycle Cost Analysis Required by Executive Order 13123," http://www1.eere.energy.gov/femp/pdfs/lcc_guide_05.pdf.
17. EPA, "Risk Management Sustainable Technology: Life Cycle Assessment (LCA)," http://www.epa.gov/nrmrl/std/lca/lca.html.
18. Joel Ann Todd and Gail Lindsey, *Planning and Conducting Integrated Design (ID) Charrettes*, Whole Building Design Guide, http://www.wbdg.org/resources/charrettes.php.
19. BREEAM, http://www.breeam.org/.
20. Green Globes, http://www.greenglobes.com/.
21. ASHRAE, http://www.ashrae.org/.
22. Washington Collaborative for High Performance Schools, *Washington Sustainable Schools Protocol: Criteria for High Performance Schools*, 2010 edition, http://www.energy.idaho.gov/energyefficiency/d/washington_sustainable_schools.pdf.
23. Energy Star, http://www.energystar.gov/.
24. Forest Stewardship Council, http://www.fscus.org/.
25. Green Label/Green Label Plus, http://www.carpet-rug.org/commercial-customers/green-building-and-the-environment/green-label-plus/.

RESOURCES

2005 White Paper: Life Cycle Assessment and Sustainability. Supplement to *Building Design +
Construction,* November 2010, http://www.bdcnetwork.com/2005-white-paper-life-cycle-
assessment-and-sustainability. An in-depth look at life cycle assessment.

American Library Association. *Building Libraries and Library Additions: A Selected Annotat-
ed Bibliography: ALA Library Fact Sheet 11.* https://www.ala.org/ala/professionalresources/
libfactsheets/alalibraryfactsheet11.cfm. This fact sheet provides references to the tools, resources, and advice to help you manage your library building project, whether large or
small.

Antonelli, Monika. "The Green Library Movement: An Overview of Green Library Literature
and Actions from 1979 to the Future of Green Libraries." *EGJ: Electronic Green Journal*
(2008), http://escholarship.org/uc/item/39d3v236. A comprehensive look at the history of
green library literature.

Antonelli, Monika, and Mark McCullough. *Greening Libraries.* Los Angeles: Library Juice
Press, 2012. A collection of articles and papers that serve as a portal to understanding a wide
range of green and sustainable practices within libraries and the library profession.

ASHRAE, The American Society of Heating, Refrigerating and Air-Conditioning Engineers.
http://ashrae.org/. ASHRAE, founded in 1894, is a building technology society with more
than 50,000 members worldwide. The society and its members focus on building systems,
energy efficiency, indoor air quality, and sustainability within the industry. Through research, standards writing, publishing, and continuing education, ASHRAE shapes tomorrow's built environment today.

Center for Sustainable Economy. "Ecological Footprint." http://www.myfootprint.org/. Accessed August 27, 2012. Ecological footprint quiz.

Cullen, Scott. *Value Engineering.* Whole Building Design Guide. http://www.wbdg.org/
resources/value_engineering.php. Discusses value engineering which is a conscious and
explicit set of disciplined procedures designed to seek out optimum value for both initial and
long-term investment.

Environmental Protection Agency. *Life Cycle Assessment (LCA).* http://www.epa.gov/nrmrl/
std/lca/lca.html. An in-depth look at LCA.

Environmental Protection Agency. http://www.epa.gov/. EPA (or sometimes USEPA) is an
agency of the U.S. federal government created for the purpose of protecting human health
and the environment by writing and enforcing regulations based on laws passed by Congress.

Environmental Protection Agency. *Life Cycle Assessment (LCA).* http://www.epa.gov/nrmrl/
std/lca/lca.html. An in-depth look at LCA.

Executive Order No. 13,123. Greening the Government through Efficient Energy Management.
64 Fed. Reg. 30851. June 8, 1999 1999. http://www.wbdg.org/ccb/browse_doc.php?d=342.

Green Building Certification Institute. http://www.gbci.org/homepage.aspx. A third-party organization that provides independent oversight of professional credentialing and project
certification programs related to green building. GBCI is committed to ensuring precision in
the design, development, and implementation of measurement processes for green building
performance (through project certification) and green building practice (through professional credentials and certificates).

The Green Library. http://thegreenlibraryblog.blogspot.com/2010/01/new-book-how-green-is-
my-library.html. The Green Library blog is devoted to documenting significant activities,
events, literature, and projects that focus on increasing the efficiency with which buildings
use resources.

Integrated Design Collaborative. http://integrativedesign.net/. Experts at integrative systems
design, management processes, and cultural change guidance that are the only real way to
achieve true sustainability across an entire enterprise in a cost-effective way.

Kats, Greg. *Greening America's Schools: Costs and Benefits.* A Capital E Report. October
2006, http://www.usgbc.org/ShowFile.aspx?DocumentID=2908.

Leonard, Annie. "The Story of Stuff." YouTube video, 21:16 minutes. 2007. http://www.
youtube.com/watch?v=gLBE5QAYXp8. The subtitle of the book by the same name says it

all: How Our Obsession with Stuff Is Trashing the Planet, Our Communities, and Our Health-and a Vision for Change.

Matthiesen, Lisa Fay, and Peter Morris. *The Cost of Green Revisited: Reexamining the Feasibility and Cost of Sustainable Design in the Light of Increased Market Adoption.* Davis Langdon, 2007. http://www.davislangdon.com/USA/Research/ResearchFinder/2007-The-Cost-of-Green-Revisited/. The subtitle describes the white paper's content.

Miller, Kathryn. "Public Libraries Going Green." *ALA Editions* (2010). Going green is now a national issue, and patrons expect their library to respond in the same way many corporations have. Libraries can take a role in environmental leadership.

The National Charrette Institute. http://www.charretteinstitute.org/. The breakthrough planning tool for community transformation.

Nugent, Sarah, et al. *Living, Regenerative, and Adaptive Buildings.* Whole Building Design Guide. http://www.wbdg.org/resources/livingbuildings.php. Discusses buildings that better fit into the natural environment without taking from it.

Steven Winter Associates. *Net Zero Energy Buildings.* Whole Building Design Guide. http://www.wbdg.org/resources/netzeroenergybuildings.php. Discusses the concept of a building which produces as much energy as it uses over the course of a year.

Sustainable Building Advisor Institute. http://sbainstitute.org. The SBA Program provides a systems approach to designing, constructing, and operating high performance buildings. The SBA Program has been running for over ten years and is currently offered at 28 locations in North America. Since 1999, over 1,250 students have graduated from the course; since 2005, more than 850 graduates have passed the professional exam to earn the credential of certified sustainable building advisor (CSBA).

United Nations. *Report of the World Commission on Environment and Development: Our Common Future.* 1987. http://www.un-documents.net/wced-ocf.htm. Commonly referred to as the report of the Brundtland Commission.

U.S. Green Building Council. http://www.usgbc.org/. The U.S. Green Building Council is committed to a prosperous and sustainable future through cost-efficient and energy-saving green buildings. Our community of leaders is working to make green buildings available to everyone within a generation. Responsible for the various LEED building standards.

Vierra, Stephanie. *Biomimicry: Designing to Model Nature.* Whole Building Design Guide. http://www.wbdg.org/resources/biomimicry.php. Discusses the science and art of emulating Nature's best biological ideas to solve human problems.

Whole Building Design Guide. www.wdbg.org. A website by the National Association of Building Sciences devoted to providing information on building-related guidance, criteria, and technology from a whole buildings perspective.

WS-IDP Committee. *Whole Systems Integrated Process.* Market Transformation to Sustainability Guideline Standard. September 2006. http://www.integrativedesign.net/images/WholeSystemIntegration.pdf. A document that codifies the meaning, importance, and practice structure of an integrated design process.

Chapter Two

The Importance of Place

From the Philosophical to the Practical

Our kinship with Earth must be maintained; otherwise we will find ourselves trapped in the center of our own paved-over souls with no way out.—Terry Tempest Williams, *Finding Beauty in a Broken World* (2008)

A SENSE OF PLACE

Terry Tempest Williams's quote offers us an uncomfortable image and a dire warning. Human beings have been using up the Earth like there are other Earths to replace it. Yet, for our well-being, it is essential to be in harmony with nature and preserve our home, our *one* Earth. Scott Russell Sanders said it best in *Staying Put: Making a Home in a Restless World*:

> In belonging to a landscape, one feels a rightness, an at-homeness, a knitting of self and the world. This condition of clarity and focus, this being fully present, is akin to what the Buddhists call mindfulness, what Christian contemplatives refer to as recollection, what Quakers call centering down. I am suspicious of any philosophy that would separate this-worldly from other-worldly commitments. There is only one world, and we participate in it here and now, in our flesh and our place. [1]

A sense of place is important for the human condition. Yet there are no precise definitions of at-homeness or sense of place. Still we know that emotional connections to structures, landscape, and places on a map create a sense of place. A subjective concept, there are a variety of definitions that put focus to this concept. Here are three:

1. The National Trust for Historic Preservation offers a straightforward approach, calling sense of place "those things that add up to a feeling that a community is a special place, distinct from anywhere else."[2]
2. Kent Ryden provides a more nuanced definition that recognizes the necessity of inhabiting place: "A sense of place results gradually and unconsciously from inhabiting a landscape over time, becoming familiar with its physical properties, accruing history within its confines."[3]
3. Finally, the geographer J. B. Jackson offers this elaboration: "It is place, permanent position in both the social and topographical sense, that gives us our identity."[4]

From these slightly different perspectives, it can be seen that sense of place is primarily about the human landscape, our legacy of impact on the land, and, perhaps most importantly, memory. A number of other characteristics about sense of place have been enumerated in a Brown University thesis by Nathan James.[5] Sense of place, as outlined by James, and modified by the author, is

- Difficult to quantify and abstract—place can be difficult to locate geographically, and a particular concept of place may not transfer across political or geographic borders
- Comprised of natural features, patterns of human settlement, and social relationships—the connection between people is a key component of place
- Determined by local knowledge—while it may be possible to broadly describe place as an outsider, intimate understandings of place are best expressed by natives
- Embodied in folklore, personal narrative, and history—intimate descriptions of place rarely show up in official documents, such as those prepared by government or bureaucratic agencies, but in cultural histories and literary works
- Embodied in cultural resources— historic buildings, sites, landscapes, scenic roads, museums, watersheds, libraries (of course), and other special places of local significance

Buildings are very much a part of the human landscape. Those who have designed our best libraries understand this and design them to give their communities a sense of place, to be special places of local significance. If libraries are successfully designed, constructed, and maintained, you feel a sense of belonging as you approach the library and when you step inside. Whether your quest is to find an answer to a question, seek respite, find employment, check email, do research, or find entertainment for the mind, libraries that create a sense of place are places of learning and affirmation that bring communities together and places where their communities want to be.

Equally important to remember when selecting a site for a library in a community or on a campus is an observation by Tom Daniels: "Community design is about place making. The physical layout of the community can and should connect people with each other, with the community, and with the surrounding countryside."[6]

THE PROCESS OF SITE ASSESSMENT

A sense of place and at-homeness are key considerations when choosing a site on which to build a new library. But they are not the only reason to pay close attention to the land on which we build our buildings and the way they are built. Place-based understanding and attendant planning are vital to achieving sustainable development that protects the Earth on which we live and we the people who inhabit it.

Sustainable development differs from the usual development practices in profound ways. In fact, in standard development processes, site assessment might not take place at all. However, the principles of site assessment and the practical process are critical to the library building working harmoniously with the land on which the building will sit and the community of which it will be a part.

PROJECT GOALS

Before starting a site design process, it is important to set your library's project goals. What is it you would like to do? What would you like to achieve both with your building and your services? As you set your goals, it is important to keep the following in mind. First and foremost, the health of the ecosystem, including human life, trumps all other priorities. Land is immobile. It is located where it is, not elsewhere. Likewise, the surrounding features are the surrounding features, both the good and the bad, unless the surrounding features are human-made and you have jurisdiction over them. No two pieces of land are alike, so it is best to determine what is unique about the site in question. Moreover, land is indestructible and scarce. It will be around for a while, and more is not being made. Use the land wisely, with the least impact. Let your library exist harmoniously with the land, without damage to it. Finally, consider that the development you are envisioning will impact the land it occupies and the surrounding areas.

Specific goals, to meet your library's needs, will follow from these principles. How many people will the building serve? What is the demographic of the library clientele? How often will they visit the library? How often will they use online resources? Will the library be a community center? Will the library be an information commons? What other services might be housed in the same building? These are but a few of the questions that need discussion and answers. Remember, though, in a green library, how the services are accessed, what equipment is used, what format the collections might take, what furnishings might be used might well have different answers than if you were building a more traditional library and offering more traditional library services.

Gentle use of the land is a simple but profound concept. Simple though it may be, site planning for sustainable land use is a complex process that provides you with the figurative foundation for your green library. For this reason, it is absolutely imperative that all members of the planning team understand the sustainable site planning design process and principles.

STAKEHOLDERS AND PLANNING TEAM MEMBERS

There are many people who can influence the goal setting and site assessment and development. Many minds to one purpose will more likely produce a robust plan that avoids pitfalls and make the best use of the proposed site. Therefore, involve as many as possible, as soon as possible. Figure 2.1 is a checklist of potential stakeholders and planning team members who should be considered. Not every stakeholder may need to participate in every step in the planning process, but at a minimum, every stakeholder identified should visit the library's proposed site and should also read a draft report for input and comment.

THE PLANNING PROCESS

Once you have set your goals, you can begin the planning process. Planning must be an iterative and integrated series of processes dependent on participation from all stakeholders. As this process relates to site selection, these processes must be interconnected at different levels, between and among federal, state, regional, and local levels of government, organizations, and ecosystems. In other words, the planning team must ask: Where is the library building to be located? Is the site urban or rural? Are there several sites under consideration? What are the various codes and regulations relating to the jurisdiction in which the building is located? Given the particular site or sites, what are the state, regional, and local implications for heating, cooling, water, landscaping, stormwater, and transportation? Based on what you find, the project goals may need to be adjusted due to such things as regulations, site limitations, and the financial resources at hand.

When conducting the site assessment, there are key questions that will need answers:

Checklist of Potential Stakeholders

(Print and Use)

___   Client/owner (librarian)
___   Board members/administrators
___   Library patrons/friends/faculty
___   Neighborhood focus groups
___   Architect
___   Civil engineer
___   Geotechnical expert
___   Site planner
___   Sustainable building advisor
___   Rating system professional (e.g., LEED AP)
___   Transportation planner
___   Financial institution representative
___   Surveyor
___   Environmental specialists
___   Real estate agent
___   Broker
___   Attorney
___   Foundation representatives
___   Contractor (if identified)
___   Public artists
___   Landscape architect
___   Structural engineer
___   Planners
___   Partners (located in the building)
___   Interior designer
___   Other (appropriate to your circumstances)

Figure 2.1.   Checklist of potential stakeholders.

- What are the physical characteristics of the site and its surroundings?
- Will the proposed use of this space for a library fit?
- What are the regulations (whether city, county, etc.) that will apply?
- What are the anticipated infrastructure requirements?
- What are the plans for the use of the surrounding properties?
- Does the site have particular issues? For instance, is it a brownfield (a piece of land that was used as an industrial or commercial site), a wetland, and so on?

There is a tendency to want to skip over or lightly address the various components of site assessment. Fight that tendency if it happens. These important steps, when skipped, can cause untold problems later on. Rather, approach this phase of the building process with interest, enthusiasm, and definite purpose. Find the information you need, apply the information to the library that would best fit on the land, and adjust your goals as required based on what you learned.

THE EIGHT STEPS OF SITE ANALYSIS

There are eight basic steps in site analysis.

1. Compile published information, reports, and data about the site.

Check with whatever governmental entities have jurisdiction over the property or properties in question. What types of reports, data, and regulations apply to the site? Figure 2.2 is a checklist of types of reports, documents, and information that might be available.

2. Conduct community research.

What were previous uses of the property? Is this a brownfield? Is it a wetland? Are there other water features? Is there a need to honor a past use that reflects the area's cultural history? How can this project retain or create open space? Figure 2.3 lists some community considerations.

3. Select a location.

If you have several site alternatives, select a location that best fits the community you wish to serve and least impacts the environment. Strategies in sustainable site selection include the following:

- Transit oriented development (TOD). TOD is one of the strategies that is most logical to consider for a library. Select a site that is close to transit

Checklist of Municipal, County, and Other Government Documents and Records

(Print and Use)

____   Aerials from various agencies (e.g., DOT, DNR)

____   Army Corp of Engineers (wetlands, floodplains)

____   Comprehensive plans

____   Critical area maps/building land inventories

____   Environmental Protection Agency (EPA) documents

____   US Forest Service (USFS) maps

____   US Geological Survey (USGS) maps

____   Insurance maps

____   National Flood Insurance maps

____   National wetland inventory maps

____   Planimetric maps

____   Soil conservation manuals

____   Surveys of record

____   Tax or assessor maps

____   Title reports (easements, etc.)

____   Topographic maps

____   Utility maps

____   Zoning maps/ordinances

____   Private sources

____   Other (check area libraries for documents that be needed)

Figure 2.2.   Checklist of municipal, county, and other government documents and records.

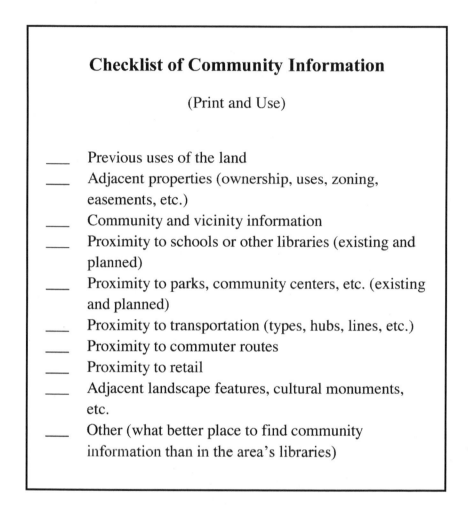

Checklist of Community Information

(Print and Use)

____   Previous uses of the land

____   Adjacent properties (ownership, uses, zoning, easements, etc.)

____   Community and vicinity information

____   Proximity to schools or other libraries (existing and planned)

____   Proximity to parks, community centers, etc. (existing and planned)

____   Proximity to transportation (types, hubs, lines, etc.)

____   Proximity to commuter routes

____   Proximity to retail

____   Adjacent landscape features, cultural monuments, etc.

____   Other (what better place to find community information than in the area's libraries)

Figure 2.3.   Checklist of community information.

hubs, such as a bus transit center or a light rail station. This strategy will place the library in a high-density area and allow library patrons the most transportation choices. TOD will allow patrons to visit the library without bringing a car, thus reducing the need for parking, and allowing people who do not own a car to come to the library.

• Low impact development (LID). As defined by the EPA, LID is "an approach to land development (or re-development) that works with nature to manage stormwater as close to its source as possible. LID employs principles such as preserving and recreating natural landscape features minimizing imperviousness to create functional and appealing site drainage that treat stormwater as a resource rather than a waste product." There are many practices that have been used to adhere to these principles such as bioretention facilities, rain gardens, vegetated rooftops, rain barrels, and permeable pavements.[7] Some of these approaches can work well for a library building. Rain gardens, vegetated rooftops, and bioretention facilities can be part of a tranquil landscape. Permeably paved parking lots can reduce the amount of water that goes immediately to stormwater treatment, which in turn reduces the load on the stormwater treatment facilities and reduces the library's stormwater treatment bill.

- Redevelopment. Redevelopment strategies include infill and rehabilitating a brownfield. Essentially you may be able to recycle land, rather than opt to disturb an undeveloped area. Certainly clean-up costs must be considered, but there may be funds available to offset such costs. This may mean that you can locate the library in a high-density area or become the anchor needed to help gentrify the community. Consider city or county plans including residential options, commercial endeavors, and what the neighborhood demographics are and will be.
- Conservation development. Also known as conservation design, conservation development employs controlled growth and sustainable development, while maximizing and protecting natural environmental features in perpetuity. This includes preserving open space landscape, protecting farmland or natural wildlife habitats, and maintaining the character of rural areas.
- Community energy planning. Although relatively new in communities, community energy planning is "a means of reviewing and evaluating community design options for a more efficient and sustainable use of energy." Rather than rely on a single company in a single location to supply the community's energy, the community comes together to develop an energy supply, most often using renewable energy sources. "Since energy use is a component of every community project, planning for energy and resource use can help communities achieve long-term sustainability. Taking steps to conserve energy and use energy more efficiently, while also developing renewable resources within the communities, will reduce the environmental impacts of energy use."[8]

4. Conduct field research.

Visit the site or potential sites. The team needs to conduct a practical, feet-on-the-ground site assessment, including microclimate, building orientation, energy options, vegetation, water, wildlife, air flow, traffic patterns surrounding the property, transportation options, surrounding services, noise factors, and contamination. This sort of assessment should not be determined simply by consulting maps or using a global positioning system (GPS). Everyone on the team should visit in person, preferably at the same time, in order to interact and discuss the site's attributes together while on site. Either fill out one assessment form together while on the site, or fill out the forms separately and compare them at your next meeting.

When visiting the site, use a formal site assessment instrument. Figure 2.4 shows one such instrument from One World Design Architecture.[9]

There are also site assessment instruments available on the Internet and elsewhere that more or less cover the aspects of site planning that have been discussed here. Pick one that is comprehensive and most appropriate to your site. For example, you might want to use Cornell University's Site Assessment Checklist[10] and its companion instructions, Instructions for Completing the Site Assessment.[11]

As you may note, even the assessment instruments that look complete, such as Cornell's, could be missing factors that are key to your particular assessment. For instance, the Cornell checklist does not list noise as one of the factors to be considered. Is the land close to a freeway, well-trafficked bridge, or city street? Is the land in an airplane flight path? What are the transportation options? What are the implications that come from the answers to such questions? That is why it is essential to walk the property, to physically experience the place. Whatever site assessment instrument you might use, consider what the instrument asks, but also take note about the things of significance to your library project that might not be included.

5. Use rating systems.

It is also important for the planning team to become familiar with the approaches that the different rating systems such as LEED® use and how these rating systems relate to site assessment. Will your project apply one of these systems? It is best to know this from the beginning, because, though similar, the emphasis of each system may differ.

6. Consider alternatives.

Once you have gathered all the information, use an iterative approach. Develop different responses to site conditions and compare. Sometimes it may appear that the steps are overlapping, which is fine, as long as all the steps are completed.

7. Analyze data and produce your report.

Review and correlate data from published documents and from community and field research. The written report includes the answers to the questions posed above. The presentation should use both text and graphics, often in-

Site Analysis Data Collection

Parcel Shape and Access (locate boundaries)

_____
_____
_____

Views (document with photos)

_____
_____
_____

Surrounding Neighborhood and Architectural Context
(massing, construction type, materials, documented with
photos)

_____
_____
_____

Topography

_____
_____
_____

Water (ground water and surface runoff)

_____
_____
_____

Access and Transportation

_____
_____
_____

Circulation Patterns (pedestrian, cars, bikes)

_____
_____
_____

Vegetation and Plants Inventory

Figure 2.4. Site analysis data collection form. Reprinted with permission, One World Design Architecture.

_____
_____
_____

Animals and Habitat

_____
_____
_____

Soil (texture, smell, load bearing and drainage capacities)

_____
_____
_____

Air Quality

_____
_____
_____

Air Movement

_____
_____
_____

Solar Access

_____
_____
_____

Your Gut Reaction

_____
_____
_____

Site analysis data collection form (*continued*).

cluding base maps, "layers," and composites. The report identifies development constraints and also suggests opportunities.

8. Distribute the final report to all those who need a copy on your library planning team.

This is the final step. Make sure all stakeholders are included in the distribution.

GREEN FOOTSTEP: A CARBON EMISSIONS TOOL

Although there are many ratings systems that you may use in step 5, one in particular deserves special mention. The Rocky Mountain Institute has developed Green Footstep, an assessment tool to determine how much your new library building or renovation will contribute to global warming. It is an online assessment instrument that can help to determine design targets needed to move your library project closer to or achieve carbon neutrality, net zero site energy, and other goals. Architects, engineers, librarians, and others on your team can use this tool. It will calculate and report your greenhouse gas emissions from site development to construction and building operation.

In terms of site selection, this tool can be helpful in projecting the carbon emissions as a result of site development by comparing the native (pre-development) carbon storage of the site to the projected storage after the site is developed. Site development typically results in a net positive carbon flow from the earth to the atmosphere (i.e., greenhouse gas emissions). The Institute explains greenhouse gas emissions using these examples. "Forests in Africa are becoming smaller due to increased consumption of wood for cooking. Also, rain forests in South America are being converted to farmland that stores much less carbon."[12] Using the same method developed by the Intergovernmental Panel on Climate Change[13] to account for this depletion in carbon storage, it is possible to calculate the emissions associated with land development for buildings and urbanization.

Green Footstep is a tool that points out the importance of connecting all the phases of building from design to site development to construction to operation. If you are to truly understand the totality of the building's effect on climate change, you will need to begin to use it at the point of site selection, before any development occurs. And, perhaps, as you register the greenhouse gas emissions, you can modify your plans to lessen the library's impact on the environment. You will continue to use it during the remaining steps, from building to operation, but if you don't begin to use it during the first phase of the process, the results will not be inclusive and you will not be able to adjust your strategies to minimize the library's negative impact on the environment.

EXAMPLES

Although each site is unique, offering its own promise and challenges, here is an example of a site that took advantage of and fit into its environment. This is an example of a library that expresses the best of the city's culture.

Andrew Michler, in his article on Minneapolis's Central Library, notes that the library links the arts district to the west and a major shopping and business district to the east. Here are a few excerpts from Michler's article that speak to the library's connection to the place and the people it serves:

> The striking design is centered around the huge atrium and the projecting cantilevered awnings on either end. The jutting "wings" are welcoming features that invite the community to come on in and take a look.
>
> Inside is a main lobby, where light scoops fill five open floors with natural illumination. The interior has no supporting walls so the spaces can be adapted to whatever current and future needs dictate. The light elements such as the self-supporting stair and glass railings and elevator makes the interior feel very much connected.
>
> Local Minnesota limestone is layered in between the exterior glass plates as well as the interior floors, giving the library a sense of place. [14]

The job of your project design team is to choose a site that blends well with the library building and reflects the community's pride, culture, and commitment.

A second example of site selection is the Westhampton Free Library in Westhampton Beach, New York. It was awarded LEED Gold by the U.S. Green Building Council. The library chose to use the land where the library had been located previously, plus develop the adjacent land previously used for a hardware store. The land where the hardware store had been located was declared a brownfield site and needed mitigation. By using the brownfield site, the library contributed by removing toxins from their community.

Here are the other site-specific features of the Westhampton Free Library:

- It is located near people and businesses.
- It is easier to access the facility with parking spots and connections to other lots. A spot was also reserved for low-emitting or fuel efficient vehicle.
- There are bike racks.
- The design manages 100 percent of the stormwater runoff.
- It remove 100 percent of the suspended solids in the runoff.
- Light pollution from the library is limited.

There are many elements that recommend this library for further study. One is that they began planning with a design charrette where participants from the public, staff, board, and professionals worked on developing design concepts and strategies. These were delivered to the architect and a schematic drawing, elevations, and some other work were then delivered to the board. The board approved the plan, and all of this was done well before a public referendum, which passed and allowed for the financing of the project.[15]

YOUR PROJECT NOTES

1. Who are your stakeholders? Who will be members of your planning team? Who needs to be included? How will you organize your initial charrette?

2. Have you considered whether or not you will use a rating system, such as LEED? Which one have you selected, if any?

3. Have you set your overall planning goals for your new building, your renovation, or your sustainable additions to your existing building? How might the site enhance or detract from these plans?

4. What community information is pertinent to your project? Where might it be obtained? Don't forget your local library, or your own library, as a resource for such reports and information!

5. What agencies and information sources are pertinent to your project? Again, consider what information your local library, or your own library, might have.

6. What site assessment instrument will you use? When can you schedule the site visit? What, particularly, do you want to check when at the site? What did you learn by walking the site? How can you preserve or create open space on the site?

7. Consider the various ways the site could be used? How might the library be sited? What are the alternatives? How might the planning team choose between the alternatives?

8. Did everyone have input to the report? Did everyone have the chance to comment on the draft report? How will final decisions be made by the stake-holders?

9. To whom should the final report be distributed? When? Who needs this information in order to be sure the project stays on track?

NOTES

1. "An Excerpt from Staying Put: Making a Home in a Restless World by Scott Russell Sanders," Spirituality and Practice: Resources for Spiritual Journeys, http://www.spiritualityandpractice.com/books/excerpts.php?id=20920.

2. S. M. Stokes, A. E. Watson, and S. S. Mastran, *Saving America's Countryside: A Guide to Rural Conservation*, 2nd ed. (Baltimore: Johns Hopkins University Press, 1997), 192.

3. Kent C. Ryden, *Mapping the Invisible Landscape: Folklore, Writing and the Sense of Place* (Iowa City: University of Iowa Press, 1993), 38.

4. John Brinckerhoff Jackson, *Discovering the Vernacular Landscape* (New Haven, CT: Yale University Press),152.

5. James Nathan, Mapping the Sense of Place: Using GIS and the Internet to Produce a Cultural Resource Inventory for South Kingstown, RI (Brown University, 2001), http://envstudies.brown.edu/oldsite/Thesis/2001/james/index.html.

6. Tom Daniels, *When City and County Collide: Managing Growth in the Metropolitan Fringe* (Washington, DC: Island Press, 1999), 87.

7. Environmental Protection Agency (EPA), *Low Impact Development (LID),* http://water.epa.gov/polwaste/green/index.cfm.

8. Oregon Department of Energy, Community Energy Planning Tool, March 18, 2008, http://www.oregon.gov/energy/GBLWRM/docs/CommunityEnergyPlanningTool.pdf.

9. Reprinted with permission, Kelly Lerner, One World Design Architecture, Spokane, WA, http://www.one-world-design.com/.

10. Cornell University, "Site Assessment Checklist," http://www.hort.cornell.edu/uhi/outreach/recurbtree/pdfs/04sitelist.pdf.

11. Cornell University, "Completing the Site Assessment Checklist," 2012, http://www.hort.cornell.edu/uhi/outreach/recurbtree/pdfs/05compsite.pdf.

12. Green Footstep, http://www.greenfootstep.org/.

13. Intergovernmental Panel on Climate Change, http://www.ipcc.ch/.

14. Andrew Michler, "Green-Roofed Minneapolis Central Library Is a Civic Lesson on Eco Design," *Inhabitat*, May 25, 2011, http://inhabitat.com/green-roofed-minneapolis-central-library-is-a-civic-lesson-on-eco-design/.

15. Westhampton Free Library, "Library," http://westhamptonlibrary.net/pages/building.aspx.

RESOURCES

American Planning Association. www.planning.org/. APA is an independent, not-for-profit educational organization that provides leadership in the development of vital communities.

Building Soil. http://www.buildingsoil.org/. Builders, developers, and landscapers are adopting practices that preserve and improve the soil on building sites, grow healthier landscapes, and protect waterways. Local governments are beginning to require these practices.

Center for Livable Communities. www.lgc.org/center. The Center for Livable Communities is a national initiative of the Local Government Commission, which is a nonprofit, nonpartisan, membership organization of elected officials, city and county staff, and other interested individuals throughout California and other states.

Congress for New Urbanism. www.cnu.org/. The Congress for New Urbanism (CNU) is the leading organization promoting walkable, mixed-use neighborhood development, sustainable communities, and healthier living conditions.

Council on Library and Information Resources. *Library as Place: Rethinking Roles, Rethinking Space*. 2005. A look at the role of the academic library as reflected in its space. It is up to the reader to interpret in a green light.

EPA, Office of Transportation and Air Quality. www.epa.gov/oms/. EPA's Office of Transportation and Air Quality protects public health and the environment by regulating air pollution

from motor vehicles, engines, and the fuels used to operate them and by encouraging travel
choices that minimize emissions.

EPA Smart Growth. www.epa.gov/dced/. Smart Growth is an EPA initiative that provides an
introduction and detailed information on smart growth plus news, publications, and policies.

New Urbanism. www.newurbanism.org/. New urbanism is the revival of our lost art of place-
making and promotes the creation and restoration of compact, walkable, mixed-use cities,
towns, and villages.

NOAA Satellite and Information Service. www.ncdc.noaa.gov/. New access to climate data
online.

Powers of Ten. YouTube video. http://www.youtube.com/watch?v=0fKBhvDjuy0. This You-
Tube video takes you on an adventure in magnitudes.

Smart Growth America. www.smartgrowthamerica.org/. A nationwide coalition making neighborhoods better together.

U.S. Department of Agriculture, Natural Resources Conservation Service. http://www.nrcs.
usda.gov/wps/portal/nrcs/main/national/home. The goal of the NRCS is not just a sustainable, nutritious, abundant food supply, but also thriving ecosystems that support a diversity
of life.

U.S. Department of Agriculture, National Resources Conservation Service, Wind Rose Center.
http://www.wcc.nrcs.usda.gov/climate/windrose.html. This site has a directory of wind rose
plot images organized by state and climate station name.

Weather Underground. www.wunderground.com/. Weather Underground provides local and
long range weather forecasts, weather reports, maps, and tropical weather conditions for
locations worldwide.

Chapter Three

Energy and Lighting

The greatest opportunities for saving costs over the life of a building occur at the beginning of the design process.—AIA Energy Design Handbook

WHAT IS ENERGY AND WHERE DOES IT COME FROM?

Energy is often defined as the ability to do work.[1] Energy causes things to happen. It gives us light. It cooks our food. It warms us and our buildings. It keeps our milk cold. It cools us and our buildings. It runs our equipment. It powers our vehicles. It makes us grow and move and think. Energy is the power to change things.

Energy can be found in a number of forms. It can be chemical energy, electrical energy, heat (thermal energy), light (radiant energy), mechanical energy, or nuclear energy. There are two types of energy sources: renewable and nonrenewable. Renewable energy includes wind, geothermal, and solar. Nonrenewable energy comes from fossil fuels including coal, oil, and gas. These fossil fuels are being used far faster than they are being created, and when used they are releasing greenhouse gases that are contributing significantly to climate change.

CLIMATE CHANGE

Climate change is a reality. Today, our world is hotter than it has been in two thousand years. If this current trend continues, the global temperature will likely climb higher than at any time in the past two million years. The continual warming cannot be explained by the natural mechanisms that caused previous warm periods. There is a broad scientific consensus that humanity is largely responsible for this change and that the choices we make today will decide the climate of the future.

It is hard not to see the results of our reliance on fossil fuels. Examples abound. The full impact of the 2010 BP Deepwater Horizon disaster in the Gulf of Mexico may take a generation to reveal itself. Recently the Great Plains have experienced storms reminiscent of the 1930s Dust Bowl. Superstorm Sandy devastated parts of the east coast of the United States in 2012. Around the country, communities face devastating levels of water and air pollution as a result of coal-burning power plants, which produce millions of tons of toxic sludge and smoke each year.

Fossil fuels account for more than 80 percent of U.S. climate change pollution. Yet with current technology, renewable energy sources like wind, solar, and geothermal can provide 96 percent of our electricity and 98 percent of our total heating demand—accounting for almost all of our primary energy demand.[2]

THREE TYPES OF ENERGY

Renewable Energy

Renewable energy includes resources that rely on sources that restore themselves over short periods of time and do not diminish. Such sources include the sun, wind, moving water, organic plant and waste material (biomass), and the Earth's heat (geothermal). Some renewable energy technologies do have an impact on the environment, albeit small. For example, large hydroelectric dams can negatively affect fisheries and land use.[3]

Green Power

Green power is a subset of renewable energy. EPA defines green power as "electricity produced from solar, wind, geothermal, biogas, biomass, and low-impact small hydroelectric sources."[4] Currently consumers do not purchase electricity directly from green power sources. Instead, consumer green power is an agreement between the consumer and the utility company that the company will use some portion of the revenue collected to invest in renewables and clean energy technologies. This use of green power is indirect but real. Green power is also generated and used on-site—usually in small amounts—by solar (photovoltaic) or wind systems.

Conventional Power

Conventional power includes the combustion of fossil fuels (coal, natural gas, and oil) and the nuclear fission of uranium. Fossil fuels have environmental costs from mining, drilling, and extraction, and they emit greenhouse gases and air pollution during combustion.[5] Nuclear power generation emits no greenhouse gases during power generation. However, it does require mining, extraction, and very long-term radioactive waste storage.

BUILDING ENVELOPE

One of the most important concepts in sustainable energy in buildings is that of the building envelope. The building envelope encompasses the entire exterior surface of a building, including walls, doors, and windows, which enclose, or *envelop*, the interior spaces. The goal of sustainable practices regarding the building envelope is to keep water out and allow thermal control within. Weaknesses in the building envelope can result in several undesirable results: moisture infiltration, often leading to mold and mildew; damage caused by wind loads; high energy costs; ongoing maintenance problems; and failure of one or more architectural and engineering building systems. The envelope determines the thermal interaction with the outdoors, the availability of daylighting that comes inside, the psychological connection to nature (out-of-doors), and the many aspects of occupant comfort. (See also chapter 5, "Indoor Environmental Quality.")

Building envelope materials include flashing, roofing material, insulation, and windows. Each of these elements has a wide range of choices that offer both durability and lower maintenance dependence, in part, on local climate and the availability of materials. The materials should be chosen based on performance over the life of the library building.

The methods and construction techniques of the enclosure have a huge influence on the performance of your library. With so many advances in manufacturing processes and new materials and technologies on the market, along with updated building codes and testing criteria, the knowledge base for effective building envelope design is constantly changing and expanding.[6]

As stated above, the library's envelope determines the thermal interaction between the inside and outside. The library's interior will always strive to attain thermal equilibrium with the outdoors, which is, in fact, a dynamic and infinitely large temperature reservoir. The tendency for equilibrium is what accounts for heat flow in one direction or the other. The greater the temperature difference between the inside and outside, the greater the rate of heat transfer.

HEAT TRANSFER, R-VALUE, AND U-VALUE

Heat is transferred in three ways: conductively, convectively, and radiantly. These are concepts that you will need to understand when discussing the materials proposed for use in the library's envelope and in making HVAC determinations. You will also need to understand the concept of R-value and U-value.

The American Heritage Dictionary provides these three definitions for heat transfer:

- Conduction: "Conduction is the transmission or conveying of something through a medium or passage, especially the transmission of electric charge or heat through a conducting medium without perceptible motion of the medium itself."
- Convection: "Heat transfer in a gas or liquid by the circulation of currents from one region to another."
- Radiant: "Energy radiated or transmitted as rays, waves, in the form of particles."[7]

R-Value and U-Value

U-value represents the thermal conductivity for a two-dimensional surface. R-value, the reciprocal of U-value, is a measure of the capacity of a material to resist heat transfer. The higher the R-value, the better the material serves as insulation from heat transfer. R-value generally applies to insulating materials, roofs, exterior walls, and windows and doors. For example, insulation labeled R-19 would transfer 1/19 btu per hour per square foot per degree F of temperature difference.

Furthermore, when speaking of insulation, its effectiveness is not only dependent upon the resistance of the material to heat flow but also on how and where the insulation is installed. For example, insulation that is compressed will not provide its full R-value. Also, insulation must be installed properly; improper installation will allow heat to flow around the insulation through studs or joists and lessen its effectiveness.

DESIGNING SUSTAINABLE BUILDING ENERGY SYSTEMS

As stated in the quote at the beginning of the chapter, the design of the HVAC (short for heating, ventilation, air conditioning) system is the point at which the design team can make the most impact on the library's costs over the building's lifetime. Therefore, the designing of the library's energy system starts early, during the design phase. The preliminary design of the heating, ventilation, and cooling systems can be developed just as soon as the approximate size of the library, its configuration, location, orientation, and construction timelines are known, along with information regarding the availability of energy sources (both renewable and nonrenewable) and other factors.

In advance of the design itself you will need to assess both the human functional and physiological needs of the occupants and visitors to the library. These include visual comfort, thermal comfort, acoustic comfort, respiratory health, and psychological well-being. (See chapter 5, "Indoor Environmental Quality.")

You will also need to assess the local climate, including the dynamics of the Earth-sun system, the local climate (i.e., latitude, longitude, and solar azimuth),[8] any sources of climatic variations, and key climate indicators (e.g., temperature, including highs, lows, and variations; precipitation; humidity; solar radiation; wind velocities; sunshine; and cloud cover). Also find out about the opportunities regarding solar energy, wind energy, small hydropower, small geo-exchange, biomass, and wave power relative to supplying energy for your library. Be sure to obtain renewable energy data from your local utility and any local regulations that might be significant.

When assessing local climate you will likely come upon an index referred to as *degree days*. This index is derived from daily temperature observations at nearly 200 major weather stations in the contiguous United States. It is a unit for estimating the demand for energy required for heating or cooling. In the United States, the typical standard indoor temperature is 65°F (18.3°C). "For each 1°F decrease or increase from this standard in the average outside temperature one heating or cooling degree day is recorded. For example, if the average outside temperature for a day was 60°F, it records as 5 heating degree days (HDD); if it was 70°F, it records as 5 cooling degree days (CDD)."[9]

An effective energy system controls for temperature, moisture in the air (humidity), supply of outside air for ventilation, filtration of airborne particles, and air movement in occupied spaces. As you select your energy system you should be aware that designing these elements into a system is often driven more by first costs than by energy efficiency, CO_2 (carbon dioxide) emissions, and life cycle costs.

As your team begins to consider HVAC possibilities, keep an open mind about choices and encourage your team to do the same. HVAC engineers, like all of us, tend to be most comfortable with what they already know. They may shy away from the uncertainties that are associated with new technologies. This might mean that newer, more efficient technologies will be overlooked. Don't be afraid to ask questions and insist that the newer technologies be given careful consideration. Consider the merits of solar energy, wind energy, small hydropower, small geo-exchange, biomass, and wave power relative your library. Be sure to obtain renewable energy data from your local utility, state energy office, and site surveys. Verify what, if any, local information and regulations may be significant when considering newer technologies and energy sources.

With this information, you are ready to design a heating system that will meet the users' needs. Design in an integrated fashion using passive energy sources first, then renewable sources, and finally high-efficiency fossil fuel technologies, getting as close as possible to net-zero energy use.[10]

ENERGY SYSTEM DESIGN ELEMENTS

Energy system design may include more elements than might first come to mind. However, each element must be considered for the purpose of analyzing appropriate design principles and specifying appropriate equipment. Without proper consideration to all these elements, the library's energy system will not be as efficient as it might be. In the next sections, we will discuss the most important of these elements: passive solar design, HVAC, daylighting, electric lighting, plug loads (occupant electrical equipment), and domestic hot water.

Passive Solar Design

It is important to design with the sun in mind. Sunlight can provide heat, light, and shade for the well-designed library. Given a proper building site, virtually any library building can integrate passive solar design. Of course, if and how well passive design can be integrated depends on the building orientation and the location of its windows, skylights, and clerestories.

How might passive heating and cooling be integrated into the overall energy system? Passive solar heating techniques generally fall into one of three categories: direct gain, indirect gain, and isolated gain. The design does not need to be complex, but it does rely on knowledge of solar geometry, window technology, and local climate. Passive solar design, along with well-induced ventilation, reduces heating and cooling loads and attendant energy bills. It also increases spatial vitality and improves comfort. Passive solar design principles, using convection, conduction, and radiation, can accrue energy benefits, with relatively low maintenance over the lifetime of the library.

Operable windows, window overhangs, thermal mass, and thermal chimneys are common elements found in passive solar design. During cold weather, solar heat gain can add beneficial heat to a building, but that heat gain can be a problem during the warm summer months. A properly designed library can take advantage of the sun's warmth by using passive design concepts, including proper building orientation and well-designed roof overhangs or light shelves. In northern climates, a building should be oriented so the long axis runs in an east-to-west direction and the largest amount of wall surface and windows face south in order to take advantage of the winter sunlight.

Passive design also extends to ventilation. Naturally occurring ventilation happens when controlled through openings such as windows and doors or small vents. Awnings, shade screen, trellises, or climbing plants can be fitted to your library to shade a library in summer. West-facing rooms are especially prone to overheating because the low afternoon sun penetrates deeper into rooms during the hottest part of the day. Methods of shading against low east and west sun are deciduous plantings and vertical shutters or blinds. West-facing windows should be minimized or eliminated in passive solar design.

Passive solar design is not new. It has been used for centuries. What is new are building materials, methods, and software that can improve the design and integration of passive solar principles into modern residential structures.

HVAC

Once you have considered how you might be able to use passive solar heat and passive ventilation to their best advantages, you can turn to HVAC. Mechanical heating and cooling systems, known as heating, ventilation, air-conditioning (HVAC) systems, are not passive; they use electricity or burning fuel to achieve thermal comfort in buildings. They include air conditioners, boilers, chillers, heat pumps, humidifiers, dehumidifiers, radiant systems, and other types of equipment.

Nearly all modern buildings use mechanical heating and cooling. As first mentioned in chapter 1, "The Importance of Place," the building sector uses about 36 percent of all energy. While passive heating and cooling systems can do the most to reduce building energy use, well-designed mechanical systems are usually necessary for peak performance. Moreover, HVAC systems and passive systems need to work well *together* to achieve peak performance.

Because HVAC systems use electricity, planning them is a good opportunity to consider your power sources. Nonrenewable energy sources like fossil fuels are traditional sources of energy, but your team should consider renewable energy as well. The clean technology industry is expected to be a rapidly growing market and at a momentous point in terms of the expansion of technologies that will help diversify energy sources, lessen our reliance on fossil fuels, and lessen degradation of the environment. By some estimates, global investments in renewable energy infrastructure are projected to double from 2010 to 2020, reaching $395 billion annually by 2020.[11]

What are the possibilities of solar, wind, geothermal, biomass, or biodiesel for your library project? Determining which one or ones will suit the library requires a thoughtful evaluation of your specific situation, location, and long-term interests. A factual analysis of energy costs, technologies, and availability is necessary to determine what is best for your particular project. It is also important to consider the purchase of green power in order to invest in the local infrastructure for large-scale renewable energy. No matter what approach you take, the use of renewable energy for your HVAC system is worthwhile.

Types of HVAC Systems

There are several types of HVAC available for use:

- **Forced Air:** Forced air heating systems can be powered by natural gas, propane, oil, or electricity. In forced air heating, the furnace heats the air and sends it though ducts to the rooms where it come out of vents usually located at the bottom of a wall or in the floor. It loses some of its potency because it travels through ducts. Forced air heats the surrounding air. Air system temperatures are easily controlled. The ducts do not require as much insulation as do pipes, and there is no danger of leaking condensation or burst pipes.
- **Hydronic (Water):** Hydronic heating systems use boilers to heat water. The water is sent with pumps and pipes to radiators, air handling units, or thermal mass floors that absorb the heat and distribute it throughout the rooms. The heat is radiant, transferring heat to people or objects in a room, as opposed to the warming of the surrounding air as in forced-air heating. Steam heating systems are powered by oil or gas. The boiler turns water into steam and sends it to radiators. When the steam cools, it becomes water, goes back to the boiler and is heated again.
- **Geo-Exchange:** Geo-exchange systems derive heat or cool from the Earth using circulated air, water, or heat exchange fluid. They are divided into closed loop and open loop systems. The type you choose depends on many things such as your climate and soil conditions. Supplemental heating is provided by a furnace or boiler. Although the heat or cool may come from the Earth, fossil fuels are used for circulation.

HVAC System Components

The mechanical HVAC system in commercial buildings is usually centralized, rather than distributed, providing heating, cooling, ventilation, humidification, dehumidification, air cleaning, or a combination of these functions. Centralized systems are expensive, in part because of the distribution system needs customization to maximize efficiency. Depending on climate, at minimum the HVAC system will have a heating source, a cooling source, a distribution system, and controls. Heat and cool are produced in a single location (by boilers, chillers, etc.) and then distributed (by pipes, ducts, controls, etc.) to individual spaces. Some systems have more specialized parts components such as heat-recovery ventilators and thermal energy storage systems. Larger buildings may also have building management systems run with computers and specialized software.

Sustainable HVAC

As stated earlier, sustainable HVAC systems are those that have been designed early and optimally, focusing on natural and renewable energy sources; a tight, well-insulated building envelope; load reduction; the integration of appropriate, efficient components; and engineering efficiencies.

Load reduction can be accomplished by building a library that is no bigger than is needed. Consider the spaces that are needed now and those you can foresee in the future. Consider the nature of information delivery. What will be in print? What will be digital? What will be delivered to devices owned by the library? What will be delivered to patrons on their own devices? What spaces are needed for research and study? What spaces are needed for community gathering or performance? How efficient can the spaces be designed? Is it possible for a space to be used for dual purposes?

It is also important to take advantage of engineering principles and strategies such as cogeneration (the use of a heat source to simultaneously generate both electricity and heat), "fan laws" (reducing airflow velocity by a factor of two reduces power needs by a factor of eight), and a good design of pumps and pipes (big, straight, short pipes with small pumps) and other synergies.

Finally, efficient HVAC systems require commissioning and maintenance; this is covered in more detail in chapter 8, "Building Operations and Maintenance."

Daylighting

The American Institute of Architects defines daylighting as

> a design strategy that employs the available daytime exterior light to illuminate the interior of buildings. Appropriately designed daylighting brings daylight into the interior space without introducing unwanted glare and heat gain. Studies have shown the value of incorporating daylight into spaces for improved productivity and improved satisfaction with the work environment. [12]

As described by Gregg D. Ander, daylighting is "the controlled admission of natural light—direct sunlight and diffuse skylight—into a building to reduce electric lighting and saving energy."[13] By providing a direct link to the dynamic and perpetually evolving patterns of outdoor illumination, daylighting helps create a visually stimulating and productive environment for building occupants, while reducing as much as one-third of total building energy costs.

There are two systems of daylighting. Passive daylighting is a system of both collecting sunlight using nonmoving and nontracking systems such as windows, sliding glass doors, skylights, clerestories, and light tubes. The collected sunlight is further reflected deeper inside the library with elements such as light shelves. Active lighting, on the other hand, is a system that tracks or follows the sun and relies on mechanical devices to do so.

The Need for Daylight

Humans sometimes act as if they could live without natural sunlight. After all, we invented electricity and artificial lighting so we could conduct our activities indoors and at night. But natural daylight is something we cannot do without for the sake of our health and spirits.

Daylight is our fundamental source of clean personal energy. Light is a basic requirement for a healthy body. Sunlight is crucial to normal health and wellness. We absorb and use different components of sunlight through our eyes and skin. Being exposed to adequate sunlight is essential for our mental alertness and our emotional well-being. Sunlight keeps us alert, creative, and happy. Studies, along with our own common sense, show that when we are exposed to sunlight, "shoppers linger longer and buy more; students do better on tests; office workers are more productive and absent less often."[14]

Lighting and Vision

Light is the most fundamental element of vision. It provides contrast between an object and its background, enabling the eyes to send signals to the brain so that the object can be perceived. When there is not sufficient light, there is no contrast. For example, in total darkness, everything appears black. Conversely, when there is too much light, such as looking at stars in the sky during a sunny day, the stars cannot be seen. People with low vision can improve their functional vision if the lighting levels are increased. Print written with a pencil is more easily read when using a lamp. Similarly, the use of sunglasses will reduce lighting levels to improve the contrast allowing a person to see steps.

Considering that libraries are populated with computers, the possibility of glare is an important issue. Glare is a common problem for people who work on computers. It can wash out a screen, making it almost impossible to read. Contrast is also severely affected. Where there is glare, people's eyes automatically work to attempt correction, continually refocusing on the material. This occurs whether the glare is severe or so slight you may not be completely aware of it. The refocusing, however, places great strain on the muscles affecting the eye, and can lead to eyestrain. Therefore, it is important to work with your design team to locate your various functional areas of the library to use the daylight to its best advantage, diffusing it as might be necessary to use it to its best advantage.

When considering light design, you should also consider contrast, surface light level, the balance of light around the space, the color content, and the rendering of light sources. An engineer can measure light levels in terms of lumens and the level of foot-candles on a work surface.

Quality Daylighting Design

The daylighting designer uses concepts of "lighting power density (W/ft2), illuminance levels, contrast ratios, window to wall ratios, ceiling to skylight area percentages, and reduction in glare."[15] Part art and part science, a daylight designer must consider climate and geographical region, building type, and use, as well as the building orientation as big factors in designing a successfully daylit building. Designers must always apply basic lighting and building performance principles to successfully use daylighting to its best advantage.

Bird-Safe Daylighting

Glass lets light into buildings for the well-being of the occupants within. However, an issue of growing concern is the large number bird fatalities caused by glass. Recent efforts, such as the New York City Audubon's *Bird-Safe Building Guidelines* and a LEED® pilot credit, "Bird Collision Deterrence," are designed to reduce the threat of glass in the built environment.

Electric Lighting

According to Green Garage, lighting typically accounts for 17–20 percent of the energy usage in commercial buildings, second only to the energy demands of the HVAC system.[16] Given those numbers, it is important to design your library's lighting system properly. A sustainable lighting system integrates daylighting with a highly efficient electric lighting system to create efficient and healthy illumination for your library. Once the natural world has contributed as much natural light that is possible to your library given your geographic location and good design, highly efficient electric lighting is needed to supplement natural lighting to meet the required illumination levels. It goes without saying that your library will also need controls to integrate the natural with the electrical.

A lighting system is both complex and, if done correctly, elegant. The system, however designed, is composed of many parts. Both HVAC and lighting should be both lower in cost because of decreased energy use and potentially lower first cost if passive design allows some equipment to be downsized or eliminated. With your lighting designer, you can review the checklist of system parts and technical considerations in figure 3.1, keeping in mind both the needs of the occupants today and those of the future.

When designing lighting systems, keep in mind the benefits of automated management systems. Automated systems for lighting help manage energy and reduce waste. The choice of fixtures can also have a big impact on your energy usage. Fixtures are more than just decoration; they have an important impact on the efficiency and effectiveness of the lighting system. Newer, more efficient fixtures are now able to transmit upwards of 90 percent of the light's output, a big improvement on older fixtures.

Plug Loads

Plug loads consist of all electric appliances and equipment plugged into receptacles, including lighting systems that are not hard-wired. Plug loads are important contributors to energy usage, but they are difficult to plan for because they are largely dependent on occupant behavior. Once the library is built, staff may use personal heaters, fans, lamps, and other items. But the effect of plug loads can be mitigated in two ways. First, a proper design will mitigate the need for such appliances to augment heating, cooling, ventilation, or lighting. Second, when such appliances and equipment are needed, it is best to specify appliances that have an energy-efficiency rating such as Energy Star. If you want to measure the load that a particular appliance draws, you can use a plug-in kilowatt meter, a device that plugs into the wall to measure the electricity use of plug-in appliances.

Domestic Hot Water

Domestic hot water systems are needed in libraries to provide hot water to restrooms, kitchens, conference rooms, janitors' closets, and technical services areas. Energy use for domestic hot water in these areas is relatively small, less than 2 percent of the building energy use. Because the percentage is relatively small, it generally does not receive much attention in energy efficiency and conservation programs. But every unit of energy saved is important in reducing energy costs, as well as mitigating climate change.

MODELING AND DESIGN TOOLS

Both HVAC and lighting systems depend on energy. In an effort to design these systems efficiently and effectively, both for the occupants and for the environment, software tools have been developed to inform and regulate energy equipment and lighting design and use. The Department of Energy's Office of Energy Efficiency and Renewable Energy has gathered these re-

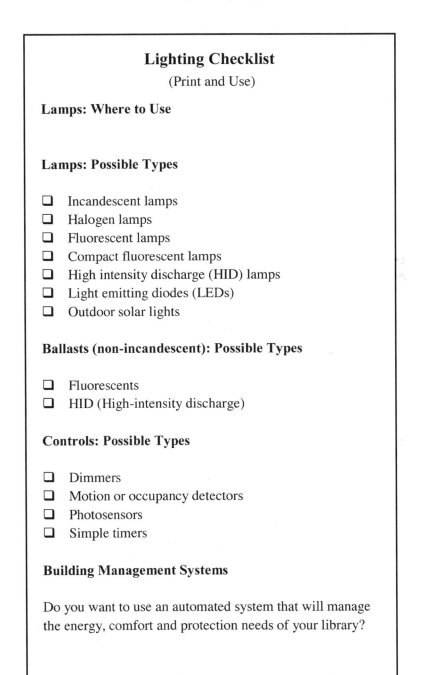

Lighting Checklist
(Print and Use)

Lamps: Where to Use

Lamps: Possible Types

- ❑ Incandescent lamps
- ❑ Halogen lamps
- ❑ Fluorescent lamps
- ❑ Compact fluorescent lamps
- ❑ High intensity discharge (HID) lamps
- ❑ Light emitting diodes (LEDs)
- ❑ Outdoor solar lights

Ballasts (non-incandescent): Possible Types

- ❑ Fluorescents
- ❑ HID (High-intensity discharge)

Controls: Possible Types

- ❑ Dimmers
- ❑ Motion or occupancy detectors
- ❑ Photosensors
- ❑ Simple timers

Building Management Systems

Do you want to use an automated system that will manage the energy, comfort and protection needs of your library?

Figure 3.1. Lighting checklist.

Fixtures

Besides the look of the fixtures, they have an important impact on the efficiency and effectiveness of the lighting system. Most fixtures transmit less, but newer, more efficient fixtures are now able to transmit upwards of 90% of the light's output.

Fixtures: Possible Types

❑ Reflectors
❑ Diffusers

Outside Lighting Considerations

❑ Solar power
❑ Security and decoration needs
❑ Avoiding light pollution

Codes

❑ Local
❑ National

Lighting checklist (*continued*).

sources together in a Building Energy Software Tools Directory.[17] This directory includes "databases, spreadsheets, component and systems analyses, and whole-building energy performance simulation programs. A short description is provided for each tool along with other information including expertise required, users, audience, input, output, computer platforms, programming language, strengths, weaknesses, technical contact, and availability."[18]

EXAMPLES

Now the second most-utilized library in the Washington, DC, system, Tenley-Friendship Branch Library is a "glowing icon." Electric and daylighting designs have been fully integrated and actively managed. The library uses daylight as the primary source of light, preserves a connection to the neighborhood,[19] and uses automated shade and light controls. The library's architecture firm describes the lighting as follows:

> The library includes a large skylit public atrium space that connects a glass volume at the public street edge which houses the reading rooms and a solid metal panel volume to the west that holds private offices. The glass volume is wrapped in angled perforated metal sunshades that regulate and filter the natural light throughout the day minimizing the need for artificial light. The glass volume is angled toward the entry to define an outdoor space along the street as well as draw visitors toward the entry.[20]

Other features include the use of solar hot water heaters, low flow plumbing fixtures, recycled materials, and a green roof. A sunken plaza to the north incorporates stepped planters that provide outdoor seating. The branch library is LEED Gold certified and, among other awards, received an IES Illumination Award of Merit in 2012.

Another great example is the Golden Gate Valley Library. The beautiful historic Beaux-Arts Golden Gate Valley Library in the Cow Hollow neighborhood of San Francisco is LEED Gold certified. As part of the San Francisco Public Library's Branch Library Improvement Program, the building was renovated with new high-performance windows, energy-efficient lighting and mechanical equipment, and a new photovoltaic system on the roof. Along with a modern addition to improve accessibility, there are some green features and renovations done related to energy and lighting.[21] It is important to note that the historic integrity of this 1917 Carnegie library was maintained and the building restored to its original grandeur.

At Parkdale Elementary in the state of Washington, 3,800 square feet of new library and computer lab space were added to an existing facility built in the 1940s. The new facilities are tucked into a U-shaped courtyard allowing the computer lab to have good daylighting while avoiding glare. The library itself features a warm, wood-finished space and magnificent views of Mount Adams across the Columbia River Gorge.

With "a goal of creating a community space and maintaining a sense of openness, the interiors focus on transparency, flexibility and warm materials."[22] The design maximizes the views of Mount Adams with floor to ceiling windows across the north end of the library. "A deliberate connection between the library and computer lab is made through windows that bring the spaces together. Sailcloth diffusers soften the light through multiple skylights in the library and computer lab, eliminating glare in the space."[23]

YOUR PROJECT NOTES

1. How will the functional and the physiological needs of your employees and patrons factor into the library's energy system design?

2. How can solar energy, including passive, or other renewables be used in your energy system design? Heating? Cooling? Lighting?

3. How might your library's use of fossil fuels be done efficiently and conservatively?

NOTES

1. Lance Winslow, "Energy Defined as The Ability to Do Work," ezinerticles.com, http://ezinearticles.com/?Energy-Defined-as-The-Ability-to-Do-Work&id=530248.

2. Greenpeace USA, "Greenpeace," http://www.greenpeace.org/usa/en/.

3. Environmental Protection Agency (EPA), "Green Power Market," United States Environmental Protection Agency, http://www.epa.gov/greenpower/gpmarket/index.htm.

4. EPA, "Green Power Market."

5. EPA, "Green Power Market."

6. "21st Century Building Envelope Systems: Merging Innovation with Technology, Sustainability, and Function," *Architectural Record*, August 2006, http://continuingeducation.construction.com/article.php?L=38&C=235.

7. *The FreeDictionary by Farlex*, accessed January 12, 2013, http://www.thefreedictionary.com/.

8. Solar Server: Online Portal to Solar Energy, http://www.solarserver.com/knowledge/lexicon/a/azimuth-angle.html.

9. Businessdictionary.com, http://www.businessdictionary.com/definition/degree-day.html.

10. Steven Winter Associates, *Net Zero Energy Buildings*. Whole Building Design Guide. July 26, 2011. http://www.wbdg.org/resources/netzeroenergybuildings.php.

11. Goldman Sachs, "The Expansion of Clean Tech and Renewables," Focus on Clean Technology and Renewables (web page), http://www.goldmansachs.com/our-thinking/focus-on/clean-technology-and-renewables/articles/expansion-of-clean-tech-and-renewables.html.

12. American Institute of Architects, "Daylighting," http://wiki.aia.org/Wiki%20Pages/Daylighting.aspx.

13. Gregg D. Ander, *Daylighting*, Whole Building Design Guide, August 24, 2013, http://www.wbdg.org/resources/daylighting.php.

14. Daylighting Collaborative, http://www.daylighting.org/what.php.

15. Daylighting Collaborative.

16. Green Garage, "Sustainable Lighting," http://greengaragedetroit.com/index.php?title=Sustainable_Lighting.

17. U.S. Department of Energy, Office of Energy Efficiency and Renewable Energy, "Building Energy Software Tools Directory," http://apps1.eere.energy.gov/buildings/tools_directory/.

18. U.S. Department of Energy, "Building Energy Software Tools Directory."

19. HLB Space, "Tenley-Friendship Neighborhood Library," http://hlblighting.com/index.php/portfolio/civic/141-tenley-friendship-library.

20. SA: Santos Architects, "New Tenley-Friendship Heights Neighborhood Library," http://santosarchitecture.com/2011/commercial/tenley-library/.

21. Bridgette Meinhold, "Golden Gate Valley Library Is a Solar-Powered LEED Gold Renovation in San Francisco," *Inhabitat*, December 28, 2012, http://inhabitat.com/golden-gate-valley-library-is-a-solar-powered-leed-gold-renovation-in-san-francisco/golden-gate-valley-library-tom-eliot-fish-paulett-taggart-architects-1/?extend=1.

22. Opsis Architecture, "Library and Computer Lab, Parkdale Elementary, Hood River, Oregon," http://www.opsisarch.com/wp-content/uploads/Case-Study_Hood-River_Parkdale.pdf.

23. Opsis Architecture, "Library and Computer Lab."

RESOURCES

Building Envelope Design Guide. Whole Building Design Guide, http://www.wbdg.org/design/envelope.php. A comprehensive guide for exterior envelope design and construction for institutional/office buildings sponsored by the National Institute of Building Sciences.

Dean, Edward T. *Daylighting Design in Libraries*. Libris Design, 2005. http://www.librisdesign.org/docs/DaylightDesignLibs.pdf. Worth the read particularly because it deals exclusively with library buildings.

Fosdick, Judy. *Passive Solar Heating*. Whole Building Design Guide. August 24, 2012. http://www.wbdg.org/resources/psheating.php. Passive solar heating is one of several design approaches collectively called passive solar design.

Graham, Carl Ian. *High-Performance HVAC*. Whole Building Design Guide. December 7, 2009. http://www.wbdg.org/resources/hvac.php. A brief but thorough guide.

New York City Audubon, "Bird-Safe Building Guidelines," http://www.nycaudubon.org/our-publications/bird-safe-buildings-guidelines. Bird safety in buildings is integral to the green sustainable building movement, and the guidelines suggest strategies that complement the LEED rating system. The guidelines also suggest ways to retrofit existing buildings.

"Passive Solar Design." SustainableSosurces.com. http://passivesolar.sustainablesources.com/. Includes a definition, commercial status, guidelines, implementation issues, and guidelines.

Sustainable by Design. "Sun Angle." http://www.susdesign.com/sunangle/. Solar angle calculator.

Sustainable Outdoor Lighting. http://www.sustainableoutdoorlighting.com/. As the website tagline states: Saving you money one light at a time.

Syska Energy Group. *HVAC Integration of the Building Envelope*. Whole Building Design Guide. December 1, 2009. http://www.wbdg.org/resources/env_hvac_integration.php. Good reading from beginning to end if you're serious about designing a highly effective HVAC system.

"Thermal Mass and R-Value: Making Sense out of a Confusing Issue," *Environmental Building News*, BuildingGreen.com, http://www.buildinggreen.com/auth/article.cfm/1998/4/1/ Thermal-Mass-and-R-value-Making-Sense-of-a-Confusing-Issue/. The title says it all.

Chapter Four

Green Materials

Only after the last tree has been cut down, only after the last river has been poisoned, only after the last fish has been caught, only then will you find that money cannot be eaten.—Cree Indian Prophecy

CONSUMPTION AND RESOURCE USE

We live on a finite earth. Because of that, consumption is part of a larger discussion of sustainability. The Worldwatch Institute tracks the continuing rise and spread of consumption and its impact on people, the planet, and profits. According to the Institute's 2011 *State of the World*, the United States, with less than 5 percent of the global population, uses about a quarter of the world's fossil fuels, burning up nearly 25 percent of the coal, 26 percent of the oil, and 27 percent of the world's natural gas. When considering the built environment, new houses in the United States were 38 percent bigger in 2002 than in 1975, despite having fewer people per household on average.[1] No matter the resource, the United States continues to *gobble* resources. According to Worldwatch,

> Calculations show that the planet has available 1.9 hectares of biologically productive land per person to supply resources and absorb wastes—yet the average person on Earth already uses 2.3 hectares worth. These "ecological footprints" range from the 9.7 hectares claimed by the average American to the 0.47 hectares used by the average Mozambican.[2]

As this last set of statistics demonstrates, there are grave inequities in consumption rates from the people of one country to the people of another. Furthermore, the overall rapid rate of consumption is leading to environmental degradation. Yet rampant consumerism does not lead to healthier, more satisfying lives. As documented by Worldwatch, the "aggressive pursuit of a mass consumption society also correlates with a decline in health indicators in many countries, as obesity, crime, and other social ills continue to surge."[3] Although the statistics may change a bit from year to year, the extent of the problem is clear. Certainly there is need for change.

That kind of data is what has propelled the interest in and commitment to sustainability. It is what has propelled people to want to build beyond codes that are often minimum standards that do not go far enough toward sustainability. There is a definite need to slow down the rate of consumption, by using space more efficiently and by reuse, recycling, and renewables. Selecting materials and products for building or renovating for a green building project means more than just choosing them based on performance, aesthetics, and cost. It means selecting products and making decisions that will reduce the environmental and health impacts of your library building. These range from big decisions, like location, to seemingly small decisions, like what adhesives or paint to use. All the materials and products can contribute to the greening process if they are chosen wisely, and the beneficial effects are cumulative. That being said, reducing the library's environmental impact requires thinking and learning about where the materials come from, how they will be used, and where the materials will go when their life in the building is done. These characteristics are worth exploring here and keeping in mind as you plan your building or renovation.

GREEN DEFINITIONS

It is important to note that there is a specialized vocabulary integral to an understanding of green materials. As your project design team discusses, researches and selects products and materials throughout the entire project, from the studs to the furniture to the cleaning products, here are some of the terms you will encounter:

- **Chain of custody:** A legal term that refers to the ability to guarantee the identity and integrity of the sample (or data) from collection to reporting of the test results.
- **Closed loop recycling:** A production system in which the waste or by-product of one process or product is used in making another product.[4]
- **Eco-labeling:** The practice of marking products with a distinctive label so that consumers know that their manufacture conforms to recognized environmental standards.[5]
- **Embodied energy:** The total energy required to produce a finished product or material, including the energy used to grow, extract, manufacture, and/or transport it to the point of use, as if the energy were incorporated

into the product or material itself. This concept is useful in determining the effectiveness of energy-producing or energy-saving devices. In other words, does the product produce or save more energy that it took to make it?

- **Environmentally preferable products:** Environmentally preferable products (EPPs), as defined by the federal government in several Executive Orders,[6] require federal agencies to purchase environmentally preferable products and services.

- **Greenwashing:** Green has become chic and profitable. It is no wonder, then, that corporations want to label their products green. However, a label does not a green product make. *Greenwashing* refers to marketing a product or material as if it met energy-saving criteria when in fact it doesn't. Dictionary.com defines it as "a superficial or insincere display of concern for the environment that is shown by an organization."[7] TerraChoice Environmental Marketing defines greenwash as "the act of misleading consumers regarding the environmental practices of a company or the environmental benefits of a product or service." TerraChoice recently released its *Seven Sins of Greenwashing* report, finding that 98 percent of products surveyed in the United Kingdom committed at least one sin. The seven sins, which are fully explicated in the report, are The Sin of the Hidden Trade-Off, The Sin of No Proof, The Sin of Vagueness, The Sin of Worshipping False Labels, The Sin of Irrelevance, The Sin of Lesser of Two Evils, and The Sin of Fibbing. Good companies with good green products will call their products *green*, but so will companies that practice the deceitful art of greenwashing. Therefore, it is important for you, the librarian and consumer, to distinguish truth from fiction, green from greenwashing.

- **Indoor environmental quality (IEQ):** According to the EPA and the National Institute for Occupational Safety and Health, the definition includes: (1) the introduction and distribution of adequate ventilation air, (2) the control of airborne contaminants, and (3) the maintenance of acceptable temperature and relative humidity. According to ASHRAE Standard 62, acceptable indoor air quality is defined as "air in which there are no known contaminants at harmful concentrations as determined by cognizant authorities and with which a substantial majority (80 percent or more) of the people exposed do not express dissatisfaction."[8] (See chapter 5, "Indoor Environmental Quality.")

- **Life cycle analysis:** The process of evaluating all of the costs of a project—environmentally and otherwise—from planning and design to construction, operation, and disposal. (See chapter 1, "The Fundamentals of Sustainable Building," where this term is discussed in some detail.)

- **Life cycle assessment:** A method for measuring environmental impacts throughout a building's or product's life cycle. (Again, see chapter 1 where this term is discussed and compared to life cycle analysis.)
- **Material Safety Data Sheet (MSDS):** OSHA-required documents supplied by manufacturers of products containing hazardous chemicals. MSDSs contain information regarding potentially significant levels of airborne contaminants, storage and handling precautions, health effects, odor description, volatility, expected products of combustion, reactivity, and procedures for spill clean-up.[9] The MSDS may be used to comply with OSHA's Hazard Communication Standard, 29 CFR 1910.1200.
- **Postconsumer recycling material:** A reclaimed waste product that has already served a purpose to a consumer and has been diverted or separated from waste management collection systems for recycling. Example: used newspaper that is made into cellulose building insulation.[10]
- **Preconsumer recycled material:** A material that is removed from production processes (including scrap, breakage, or byproducts) and reused in an alternative process before consumer distribution. Example: mineral (slag) wool, a byproduct of the steel blast furnace process, used for mineral fiber acoustical ceiling panels.[11]
- **Rapidly renewable materials:** Agricultural products, both fiber and animal, that take ten years or less to grow or raise and can be harvested in an ongoing and sustainable fashion. BuildingGreen.com has developed a list of products that fall within this definition, including types of concrete, woods, composites, and furnishings.[12]
- **Sustainable forestry practices:** Sustainable forestry practices are a moving target, varying from place to place and through time. While sustainability encompasses the concept of *sustained yield*, which refers to the continuing ability of forests to supply timber, the services that a forest provides go much farther than this. Sustainability implies the long-term maintenance of all forest functions including ecological and landscape conservation, soil protection, recreation, aesthetic values, as well as the production of timber and other forest products. Management of a forest for a single product affects the forest's ability to provide other services or products. Tradeoffs need to be made. For example, managing the forest for high levels of timber production may diminish its value as a habitat for animals.[13]

CHARACTERISTICS OF GREEN MATERIALS AND PRODUCTS

There is no precise definition for green materials or products. However, there certainly are green characteristics. And there are certainly *shades of green*. For instance, how green is a cork floor? The cork is a renewable material, but what if it were shipped from Spain? Is a tile made locally from local materials a greener option? How should the factors such as renewables and distance be weighted? There are no precise answers. Rather, it is up to your library project planning team to weigh the pros and cons and determine what products are greener and what is affordable. This makes the selection of materials for the library, from studs to stuffed furniture, an important task for the project team.

It is important to look at the materials' and products' impact on the environment during its entire life cycle from *cradle to grave*. The entire life cycle includes raw material acquisition, manufacturing, distribution, use, and disposal or end-of-life management. In addition, the evaluation of green products requires a working knowledge of these issues:

- Relevant health and environmental impact issues associated with different material types
- Government, industry, and third-party standards for green products, where they exist
- Available green products in the marketplace, including their specific green attributes, performance characteristics, appearance, and costs

At the end of this chapter, figure 4.1 provides a checklist of attributes and considerations that may be useful when considering whether or not a product or material is green. The checklist considers a product or material at different stages of its lifecycle, including material, manufacture, distribution, use, and disposal/reuse.

THE CHEMICAL COMPOSITION OF MATERIALS

Better living through chemistry?[14] Sometimes yes and sometimes no. Knowing and understanding the chemical composition of a material or product is of the utmost importance when determining whether or not it is green. Scientific advancements in material science have allowed for a better identification of the health and environmental consequences of chemicals, including the properties, structure, performance, and durability of materials, as well as the resulting hazards of a material, from their manufacture to their breakdown.

There are a number of highly controversial compounds or materials used in building that are now considered to be problematic. When you understand why the compounds are toxic, you better understand the need to identify which traditional building materials are toxic and what materials can be used as better, more sustainable replacements for use in your library project.

Some of the most well-known offenders include polyvinyl chloride, formaldehyde, volatile organic compounds, and flame retardants (belonging to a large group of chemicals known as persistent bioaccumulative toxins (PBTs). Also important to keep in mind are toxic materials that are no longer used in new buildings but may be present in existing buildings in need of renovations. These include lead (in old paint and plumbing), asbestos (in insulation, appliances, etc.) and mercury (switches, paints, thermostats, and still used in florescent and mercury-vapor lamps). It is vital to determine whether your library has any of these materials before renovation begins. It's equally important to make sure that they are removed in a manner that is safe for the environment and for the demolition workers.

BuildingGreen has published a report entitled *Avoiding Toxic Chemicals in Commercial Building Projects*[15] in which four steps for avoiding toxic chemical are outlined:

- **Step 1:** Identify the worst toxic hazards. These include carcinogens (which cause, promote, or aggravate cancer); reproductive or developmental toxicants (which can lead to birth defects, low birth weight, and functional or behavioral weaknesses); mutagens (which cause mutations or chromosome abnormalities), endocrine disruptors (which mimic or block the actions of hormones); and neurotoxicants (which affect the nervous system and brain functions).
- **Step 2:** Make sure your team is knowledgeable about these chemical hazards and use that to guide what to spec and what not to spec. (The BuildingGreen publication would be helpful here, but there are also other sources on materials specification as well.)
- **Step 3:** Study environmental product declarations, red lists, certifications, and databases to help you make informed decisions.
- **Step 4:** Collaborate as a team to educate yourselves on chemical toxicity and to avoid building product health hazards for a healthier, more environmentally friendly library.

MATERIALS ANALYSIS: USING LIFE CYCLE ASSESSMENT (LCA)

More than just a concept, life cycle assessment is an increasing viable tool for informing building design decisions. Software tools have become more user-friendly, consistent, and comparable. LCAs of both generic product categories and specific products are more available. According to the EPA, while calculating and using LCA is increasing, there are several barriers prohibiting its widespread adoption:

- Lack of awareness of the importance of using the life cycle concept
- Inaccessibility to life cycle inventory data and a measure of the quality of the data

- Lack of understanding of impact assessment methodology and identifying what type of modeling is appropriate for the specific application [16]

In the current version of LEED® (2009), credits are weighted according to LCA criteria. By applying LCA to the existing credits, the total possible score for a project was increased from 69 points (in the previous version of LEED) to 100 points (or 110 including various bonus points). The six measurement categories remain the same from the last version to the current, but the points have been reallocated according to the results of the LCA weighting. For example, the section on materials and resources has increased from 13 possible points to 14. The weighting system has been constructed in a way that if environmental and societal priorities shift, the focus of LEED could shift by adjusting weightings across the key impact categories—without requiring a complete reconfiguration of LEED. The materials and resources section in the next version of LEED, titled LEED v4, is again one of the areas that will be addressed in depth, with discussions focusing on toxic chemicals and Forest Stewardship Council (FSC) wood.

PRODUCT STANDARDS AND GUIDELINES

There are a growing number of product standards and guidelines for environmentally preferable products and services. These standards will be important in guiding your library project's team decisions. Some have been written by federal government agencies; others have been developed by third-party organizations both in the United States and around the world. The EPA website Environmentally Preferable Purchasing (EPP) [17] is a handy reference tool, including an amazing amount of information regarding green products, and is updated regularly. Of particular note is the EPP page entitled Database of Environmental Information for Products and Services. [18] The database currently includes more than 500 standards covering more than 600 product and service categories.

There is a companion EPP page for green cleaning products entitled Cleaning [19] that includes a section on standards and green products and services. [20] EPA works with a variety of nongovernmental standards developers to promote the development of voluntary consensus standards for environmentally preferable goods and services. The EPP site updates the standards and guidelines information regularly.

A BRIEF LIST OF GREEN PRODUCT DIRECTORIES, STANDARDS, AND CERTIFICATIONS

Although not a definitive list, these directories, standards, and certifications will be useful in researching green materials for your library project.

Directories

- **Declare**, http://www.declareproducts.com: The International Living Future Institute launched this database of green building products that provides a kind of "nutrition label" of product ingredients, in support of the Living Building Challenge's Red List and Appropriate Sourcing imperatives.
- **Ecolabel Index**, http://www.ecolabelindex.com: The largest global directory of ecolabels.
- **Federal Green Construction Guide for Specifiers**, http://www.wbdg.org/design/greenspec.php: To address the need for a comprehensive guide for procuring green building products and construction/renovation services within the federal government, EPA has partnered with the Federal Environmental Executive and the Whole Building Design Guide (WBDG) to develop this guide.
- **Good to Be Green**, http://g2bgreen.com/: Good to Be Green is a directory of green building products, sustainable building materials, and green building service providers. Products must be made out of recycled materials; ensure a low environmental impact during the construction, operation, and/or demolition of the building; conserve natural resources like energy, wood and water; and improve air quality.
- **Green Building Pages**, http://www.greenbuildingpages.com/: Green Building Pages is an online sustainable design and decision-making tool for building industry professionals and environmentally and socially responsible consumers.
- **GreenFormat** (Construction Specifications Institute), www.greenformat.com: Manufacturers report the attributes of their products through a comprehensive, online questionnaire. Their entries are then displayed through the GreenFormat website, where designers, constructors, and building operators can search for products that fit their projects.
- **The Green Guide**, environment.nationalgeographic.com/environment/green-guide: National Geographic's Green Guide offers staff-written reviews of a host of products ranging from appliances, home furnishings, and home improvement products to personal care and pet supplies.
- **Green Label/Green Label Plus**, http://www.carpet-rug.org/commercial-customers/green-building-and-the-environment/green-label-plus/: A voluntary industry testing program for carpet and adhesive products, estab-

lishes the highest standard for indoor air quality (IAQ) ever set by the carpet industry. The Carpet and Rug Institute (CRI) created Green Label Plus to identify carpets and adhesives that are tested by an independent, certified laboratory and meet stringent criteria for low chemical emissions.

- **GreenSpec Directory**, http://www.buildinggreen.com/ecommerce/ gs.cfm: The *Environmental Building News* product directory. The *Green-Spec Directory* lists product descriptions for over 2,100 environmentally preferable products. Products are chosen to be listed by BuildingGreen editors. They do not charge for listings or sell ads.
- **Green2Green**, http://www.green2green.org/: Green2Green features comprehensive information regarding green building products, materials, and practices. The site offers side-by-side comparisons of products using a variety of environmental, technical, and economic criteria.
- **MasterSpec**, http://www.masterspec.com/: Published by ARCOM for the American Institute of Architects (AIA), this is the preeminent master guide specification system for use on building and construction projects and design firms' office masters. It includes specification language for LEED criteria and LEED projects.
- **Multiple Chemical Sensitivities Organizations**, http://www.angelfire. com/planet/mcshelpsite/orgs.html/: A directory of associations dealing with multiple chemical sensitivities.

Certifications

- **EcoLogo**, http://www.ecologo.org/en/greenproducts/: Launched by the Canadian federal government, this website offers third-party certification of more than 7,000 environmentally preferable products. EcoLogo is North America's oldest environmental standard and certification organization (and the second oldest in the world). It is the only North American standard approved by the Global Ecolabeling Network as meeting the international ISO 14024 standard for environmental labels.
- **Green Seal**, http://www.greenseal.org/: Founded in 1989, Green Seal provides science-based environmental certification standards that are credible, transparent, and essential in an increasingly educated and competitive marketplace. Industry knowledge and standards help manufacturers, purchasers, and end users alike make responsible choices that positively impact business behavior and improve quality of life.
- **Pharos Project**, http://www.pharosproject.net/: The Pharos Project certifies green materials and services and provides an evaluation tool for green building and procurement professionals. It identifies a product's impact in the three major areas, each of which contain five to six comprehensive sets of criteria. Rather than providing a rating for a product's score against these criteria, Pharos is a lens that visually depicts a prod-

uct's strengths and weaknesses in each area, much like a wind or compass rose. The goal of this presentation is to help consumers who often have to make quick decisions about products.

- **SCS: Scientific Certification Systems**, http://www.scscertified.com/: SCS is a leading third-party provider of certification, auditing and testing services, and standards, founded in 1984. Our goal is to recognize the highest levels of performance in food safety and quality, environmental protection and social responsibility in the private and public sectors, and to stimulate continuous improvement in sustainable development.

Standards

- **The Chlorine Free Products Association (CFPA)**, http://www. chlorinefreeproducts.org/: The Chlorine Free Products Association (CFPA) is an independent not-for-profit accreditation and standard-setting organization. Our focus is promoting sustainable manufacturing practices, implementing advanced technologies free of chlorine chemistry, educating consumers on alternatives, and developing world markets for sustainability produced third-party certified products and services. The CFPA has no financial interest in any manufacturer, or company, of the products it certifies.
- **Design for the Environment—an EPA program**, http://www.epa.gov/ dfe/faqs.html: Using EPA's chemical and toxicological expertise, the Design for the Environment program applies stringent criteria for health and environmental safety in labeling products with the safest possible chemical ingredients.
- **Energy Star**, http://www.energystar.gov/: Energy Star is a joint program of the U.S. Environmental Protection Agency and the U.S. Department of Energy helping us all save money and protect the environment through energy efficient products and practices.
- **EPEAT**, http://www.epeat.net/: "EPEAT is a system to help purchasers in the public and private sectors evaluate, compare and select desktop computers, notebooks and monitors based on their environmental attributes."[21] "EPEAT also provides a clear and consistent set of performance criteria for the design of products, and provides an opportunity for manufacturers to secure market recognition for efforts to reduce the environmental impact of its products."
- **Forest Stewardship Council (FSC)**, http://www.fsc.org/: The Forest Stewardship Council sets forth principles, criteria, and standards that span economic, social, and environmental concerns. The FSC standards represent the world's strongest system for guiding forest management toward sustainable outcomes. Like the forestry profession itself, the FSC system includes stakeholders with a diverse array of perspectives on what repre-

sents a well-managed and sustainable forest. FSC standards for forest management have now been applied in over 57 countries around the world.

- **GREENGUARD**, http://www.greenguard.org: The GREENGUARD Environmental Institute (GEI) is an industry-independent, non-profit organization that oversees the GREENGUARD Certification Program. As an ANSI Authorized Standards Developer, GEI establishes acceptable indoor air standards for indoor products, environments, and buildings. GEI's mission is to improve public health and quality of life through programs that improve indoor air.
- **Health Product Declaration Open Standard**, http://www.hpdcollaborative.org/: A product chemistry disclosure tool that its developers, the Health Building Network and BuildingGreen, say will provide manufacturers with a consistent format for reporting product content and associated health information.
- **The Institute for Market Transformation to Sustainability (MTS)**, http://www.mts.sustainableproducts.com/#: SMaRT consensus sustainable product standard and SMaRT Certified Products through the MTS business alliance provides substantial global benefits for the world's products through environmental, social, and economic criteria which promote sustainability, business benefits, social equity, reuse, and climate pollution reductions.
- **NSF International**, http://www.nsf.org/: NSF International has been testing and certifying products for safety, health, and the environment for more than 65 years. As an independent, not-for-profit organization, NSF's mission is to protect public health and the environment through standards development, inspection, testing, and certification for the food, water, build/construction, retail, chemical, and health science industries. Operating in more than 120 countries, NSF is committed to protecting public health worldwide and is a World Health Organization Collaborating Centre for Food and Water Safety and Indoor Environment.
- **NSF Sustainability**, http://www.nsf.org/: NSF Sustainability draws upon this expertise in standards development, product assurance and certification, advisory services, and quality systems management to help companies green their products, operations, systems, and supply chains. NSF Sustainability, through the National Center for Sustainability Standards, has developed sustainability standards for building products and materials; furniture; carpet and flooring, fabrics; wall coverings; roofing membranes; green chemicals; and drinking water quality. NSF works with leading regulators, scientists, engineers, public health and environmental health professionals, and industry representatives to develop these transparent, consensus-based standards.

- **Standardized Test Methods Committee (STMC)**, http://www.i-itc.org/
  index.html: STMC stands for the Standardized Test Methods Committee
  of the International Imaging Technology Council. This global committee
  formed to find and promote standardized test methods for the printer cartridge industry. The test methods are used to evaluate toner printer cartridge performance. Standardized test methods make it possible to evaluate a cartridge anywhere and come up with the same test results no matter
  who tests it. Standardized tests do not specify how a cartridge must perform; they only measure it.

CRADLE TO GRAVE: DURABILITY AND DECONSTRUCTION

When speaking of green materials, construction and ensuing operations and
maintenance of your library are not the end of the story. The entire life cycle
of the building, referred to as *cradle to grave*, includes all the years of
occupancy, its durability, and its ultimate deconstruction. This concept was
coined by architect William McDonough and chemist Michael Braungart. It
is based on the ecological concept that "waste is food" and that design should
follow the intelligence of natural systems.

What is the role of planning and library building materials during the
years of operations? What contributes to the building's durability? What
materials contribute to the recycling and reuse of the building materials when
the library is finally deconstructed?

The library's durability is, of course, affected by more than the choice of
materials, no matter the importance of materials. Planning for durability
includes consideration of these elements:

- **Location:** Since it is not always possible to avoid areas of potential natural hazards, the library building needs to be designed to respond to such
  potential hazards (e.g., seismic stability bracing).
- **Architectural features:** Since water, wind, and sun all wear on buildings
  over time, consider roof design, overhangs, foundation water management, and other design elements that would mitigate any adverse issue of
  climate on the site.
- **Material selection:** Material durability has a fundamental effect on building durability. Durable materials used appropriately in library buildings
  designed and constructed with durability in mind produce environmental
  and economic benefits by slowing the rate of resource depletion, reducing
  demand pressure on natural systems, and increasing the life cycle return
  on investment (e.g., finances and energy use). Materials that can serve two
  purposes (i.e., materials synergy) will help reduce consumption. Given
  that libraries are busy places that are heavily used, durability is especially

important, whether you are considering floor coverings or furniture. Purchase well but not often. Choose styles, materials, and patterns that are timeless. Match materials carefully with use patterns.

- **Assemblies:** Keep in mind that, no matter how durable a material is, if the material is part of an assembly that fails, the material itself fails.
- **Flexibility:** A building that is designed for functional flexibility and even adaptive reuse. Build library spaces that are flexible or allow for multipurpose use. Also build library space that is able to respond, as much as possible, to changing information technology and patron needs. This means adding electrical outlets, cable trays, and so on wherever technology *might* be located.
- **Quality management:** Design, material, and assembly durability can all be compromised by substandard installation and construction detailing.

After the green library building's useful life, however long it maybe, the library building will be disassembled or deconstructed. The library should be designed, from the beginning, for its eventual deconstruction. At the point of deconstruction, it will be important to facilitate materials recovery, reuse, or recycling. This takes on added significance when you consider that presently construction uses over 40 percent of all raw materials and that demolition waste represents 25–30 percent of all solid waste.[22] If now, when building our library, we select materials that are reusable or recyclable and avoid new waste-product composite materials that are neither, we can help to reduce these numbers in the future, even if that future is for the generations to come.

EXAMPLES

Lake View Terrace Library is a branch library and multiuse facility for the city of Los Angeles. It is located in the San Fernando Valley within the Hansen Dam Recreation Area. The building program includes the library, a community room, an environmental display gallery, and an exterior courtyard.

The building plan responds to the desire expressed by the community to have a library that reflects the *rancho* tradition of the region, with interior spaces organized around an open central courtyard. A spacious main reading room stretches along the east-west axis and enjoys dramatic views of the park to the south. The building is a LEED Platinum building, the first library to have obtained such recognition. Having attained the highest ranking given by LEED, the library offers an outstanding example of what can be done in the category of green materials and products.

Here is an extract of the USGBC LEED case study for the Lake View Terrace Library:

Materials & Resources
The building shell is constructed from concrete masonry units (CMU) and engineered to last 100 years. The unit masonry is exposed on the interior to provide thermal mass as part of the building's cooling strategy. The masonry is burnished to provide an elegant finish surface and to minimize the use of paint. Low-VOC finishes are used in compliance with GS-11 and SCAQMD requirements to support indoor environmental quality goals and minimize disruption of operations caused by maintenance. Glu-laminated beams are certified by the Forest Stewardship Council (FSC). 15% of the material used contains recycled content (as per LEED calculations). Fly ash replaced 20% of the portland cement in concrete and masonry grout. Other high-recycled content materials include steel; carpet; ceiling, wall, and floor tile; and building insulation. 60% of the material came from sources within 500 miles of the building site (30% was from within 100 miles), and over half was harvested locally. Designated collection areas that accommodate recycling per City of Los Angeles requirements facilitate recycling during occupancy.

Diversion of Construction & Demolition Waste
In order for contractor payments to be approved, construction waste management and IAQ specifications required aggressive material diversion from the landfill and responsible, appropriately sequenced construction practices. Over 75% of construction waste was diverted from landfills.

Green Products Used
Stormwater Filter System

Design for Adaptability to Future Uses
The library is a model of environmentally sustainable design, a civic landmark with an enduring presence that will serve its community for generations. Built of durable masonry, glu-lam beams, and metal roofing, the building is designed for a "long life," but it is wired and ducted for flexibility and a "loose fit." Interior spaces were conceived as large rooms with diverse functions defined by furniture and equipment that can be reconfigured, as needs change. Outdoor spaces are designed for possible future incorporation into the main body of the building, or to enhance its present functionality as a place for special programs, performances, and outdoor learning.

Green Strategies

- *Plan for Materials Longevity:* Design and build components with constituent parts of equivalent longevity
- *Job Site Recycling:* Seek a waste hauler who can separate recyclables out of commingled waste; Require a waste management plan from the contractor
- *Recycling by Occupants:* Specify recycling receptacles that are accessible to the occupants
- *Toxic Upstream or Downstream Burdens:* Use true linoleum flooring
- *Greenhouse Gas Emissions from Manufacture:* Use concrete masonry units with flyash replacing a portion of the cement

- *Materials and Wildlife Habitat:* Specify bamboo flooring instead of hard-
  wood
- *Transportation of Materials:* Prefer materials that are sourced and manufactured within the local area[23]

A second example is Poudre River Public Library District's Council Tree
Library in Fort Collins, Colorado. Council Tree Library was built in an
existing shell of a retail center that was designated LEED Silver by the U.S.
Green Building Council. Therefore the library, responsible for only the interior, applied to LEED under its Commercial Interiors rating system. The
library's program to complete the library's interior was highly successful and
in 2010 it was designated as a LEED Platinum Library, Commercial Interiors. As such it is a wonderful example of what can be done with green
materials on the interior. Elements contributing to the rating include a minimum of 50 percent Forest Stewardship Council–certified wood products;
recycled materials in decorative plastic panels, chairs, and ceiling grids; low-
VOC emitting paints, adhesives, carpets, and coatings; and efficient lighting
fixtures and mechanical systems.[24]

After the Lakeview Terrace Branch Library, Council Tree was the second
library in the United States to receive the LEED Platinum designation, and
the first to have obtained Platinum under LEED Commercial Interiors.

GREEN PRODUCTS CHECKLIST

Finally, now that you know a bit more about the world of green products,
following is a checklist for you to use when researching various building
materials and products. Keep in mind that you will not answer all questions
for all products or materials because green characteristics vary greatly depending on the type of product. The green attributes of a concrete mix, for
example, might include the use of fly-ash (a post-industrial recycled content
material), while the green characteristics of an interior paint might include its
low VOC content.

As you look at one product after another, consider whether or not the
material is local, does not harm the environment, fits your library's aesthetic,
and best suits your library goals. Choices will be different from library to
library, but the checklist in figure 4.1 should help you weigh your options.

YOUR PROJECT NOTES

1. Are your team members familiar with the issues involved in green materials? What green products are most important to your library project and how

Green Products Checklist:

What Makes a Product or Material Green?

(Print and Use)

Material/Product: _____

Manufacturer/Company: _____

Source

❑ Is the material or product made from natural or (rapidly) renewable resources?

❑ Will it promote good indoor air quality (typically reduced emissions of VOCs and/or no formaldehyde)?

❑ Does it incorporate recycled content (postconsumer and/or post-industrial)?

❑ Was it salvaged from existing or demolished buildings for reuse?

❑ Is it free from CFCs, HCFCs, and other ozone-depleting substances?

❑ Is it free from highly toxic chemicals, and does its production not result in highly toxic byproducts?

❑ Is it obtained from local resources and manufacturers?

❑ Is it durable and have low maintenance requirements?

❑ What is its chemical composition?

❑ Does the manufacturer have a written, working environmental policy in place? Is it easy to find on the manufacturer's website or product literature?

Figure 4.1.   Green products checklist.

Manufacture

❑ Does the manufacturer's environmental policy strive to make important improvements in manufacturing, reducing and reusing first, then recycling?

❑ Does the manufacturer comply with their industry's voluntary testing programs?

❑ Does the manufacturing process release harmful substances?

❑ Are adhesives or coatings needed to make the product viable? If so, which are being used?

❑ Is the manufacturing process energy efficient?

❑ Does the material or product have low embodied energy (the energy required to produce or transport the item)?

❑ What is its first cost?

❑ What are its service/maintenance requirements?

❑ Does the product or material have any certifications or eco-labels?

Distribution

❑ Is the product or material manufactured and distributed locally, or is it transported long distances?

Use

❑ Was the material or product salvaged from existing or demolished buildings for reuse?

Disposal

❑ Is the material or product readily recycled?

❑ Is the material or product easily reused (either whole or in part?)

❑ Is it biodegradable?

❑ Can it be reused or recycled?

❑ Can the product be returned to the manufacturer at the end of its useful life?

Green products checklist (*continued*).

will you go about selecting them? What committee or individual "expert" will assume the task of vetting materials used in the project?

2. What local sustainable products can you use that will enhance the library's sense of place? Which are recyclable? Which are rapidly renewable?

3. What recycled materials, especially materials from an earlier library or local building, can be used in your project to enhance the library's sense of place?

4. What codes govern your library building or renovation, and why is it better to build beyond code when building or renovating a library in a sustainable way? How will you ensure that this can and will happen with your project?

NOTES

1. Worldwatch Institute, "The State of Consumption Today, 2011," http://www.worldwatch.org/node/810.
2. Worldwatch Institute, "The State of Consumption Today, 2011."
3. Worldwatch Institute, "The State of Consumption Today, 2011."
4. "Closed Loop Recycling Definition," *Business Terms Dictionary*, http://www.businesstermsdictionary.com/terms/66356-closed-loop-recycling.html.
5. Oxford Dictionaries, http://oxforddictionaries.com/definition/english/eco--labelling.
6. Environmental Protection Agency (EPA), "Environmentally Preferable Purchasing (EEP): Executive Orders," http://www.epa.gov/epp/pubs/guidance/executiveorders.htm.
7. dictionary.com, http://dictionary.reference.com/browse/greenwash.
8. EPA, "Environmentally Preferable Purchasing (EEP): Executive Orders."

9. John Amatrula, *Evaluating and Selecting Green Products*, Whole Building Design Guide, http://www.wbdg.org/resources/greenproducts.php.

10. Amatrula, "Evaluating and Selecting Green Products."

11. Amatrula, "Evaluating and Selecting Green Products."

12. Building Green, "Rapidly Renewable Materials," http://www.buildinggreen.com/auth/productsByLeed.cfm?LEEDCreditID=28.

13. wiseGEEK, "What Is Sustainable Forestry," http://www.wisegeek.com/what-is-sustainable-forestry.htm.

14. The phrase "Better living through chemistry" is a variant of a DuPont advertising slogan, Better Things for Better Living . . . Through Chemistry. The slogan was adopted by DuPont in 1935 and used as such until 1982.

15. Building Green, *Avoiding Toxic Chemicals in Commercial Building Projects*, http://www2.buildinggreen.com/guidance/Avoid-Toxic-Chemicals-in-Buildings?__utma=1.1957849404.1344658325.1344658325.1345002843.2&__utmb=1.1.10.1345002843&__utmc=1&__utmx=-&__utmz=1.1345002843.2.2.utmcsr=yahoo|utmccn=%28organic%29|utmcmd=organic|utmctr=toxic%20chemicals%20building%20materials&__utmv=-&__utmk=134354673. Available for purchase from this site.

16. EPA, "LCA Resources," http://www.epa.gov/nrmrl/std/lca/resources.html.

17. EPA, "Environmentally Preferable Purchasing (EPP)."

18. EPA, "Environmentally Preferable Purchasing (EPP): Database on Environmentally Preferable Purchasing," http://yosemite.epa.gov/oppt/eppstand2.nsf.

19. EPA, "Environmentally Preferable Purchasing (EPP): Cleaning."

20. EPA, "Environmentally Preferable Purchasing (EPP): Information on Standards for Green Products and Services," http://www.epa.gov/epp/pubs/guidance/standards.htm.

21. http://www.zerowaste.org/epeat_devel/faq.htm#1.

22. Earth911, "EPA Estimates 170 Million Tons of Yearly Construction, Demolition Debris," http://earth911.com/news/2009/04/17/epa-estimates-170-million-tons-of-yearly-construction-demolition-debris/.

23. USGBC, "LEED Projects and Case Studies Directory: Lake View Terrace Library," http://leedcasestudies.usgbc.org/overview.cfm?ProjectID=289.

24. American Libraries, "Green Libraries: Poudre River Public Library District, Council Tree Library, Fort Collins, Colorado," *American Libraries*, http://americanlibrariesmagazine.org/content/green-libraries-poudre-river-public-library-district-council-tree-library-fort-collins-color.

RESOURCES

Athena Sustainable Materials Institute. http://www.athenasmi.ca/. A membership-based, nonprofit, research collaborative bringing life cycle assessment to the construction sector.

Building Green. "Environmental Resource Guide: Environmental Building News." BuildingGreen.com. http://www.buildinggreen.com/auth/article.cfm/1992/11/1/Environmental-Resource-Guide/. "The backbone of the ERG is the materials assessments, including life cycle analyses and detailed reports about various building materials from an environmental perspective." A subscription service.

Consumer Product Safety Commission. "An Update on Formaldehyde—1997 revision." http://www.cpsc.gov/CPSCPUB/PUBS/725.html. Information regarding formaldehyde, what it is, its effects, and how to mitigate.

Consumer Reports. Greener Choices. http://www.greenerchoices.org/. Products for a better planet, as per Consumer Report's tag line.

Durodie, Bill. "Poisonous Propaganda: Global Echoes of an Anti-Vinyl Agenda." Competitive Enterprise Institute. http://cei.org/studies-issue-analysis/poisonous-propaganda-global-echoes-anti-vinyl-agenda. The subtitle of this study says it all.

Environmental Protection Agency. "Choosing Green Materials and Products." http://www.epa.gov/greenhomes/SmarterMaterialChoices.htm. Valuable information although focused on green products for the home.

"Flame Retardants under Fire: Environmental Building News." BuildingGreen.com. http://www.buildinggreen.com/auth/article.cfm/2004/6/1/Flame-Retardants-Under-Fire/. The pros and cons of brominated flame retardants.

"Formaldehyde: Environmental, Health and Safety Information." http://www.ehso.com/chem_formaldehyde.htm. The subtitle summarizes the document.

Green Concrete. "Concrete Solutions for Sustainable Development." http://www.greenconcrete.info/. Information about concrete as a green product over the building's life cycle.

"The Greenwash Guide." Futerra, 2degrees. http://www.2degreesnetwork.com/groups/all-2degrees-members/resour)ces/greenwash-guide_3/. Greenwashing is with us, so we must learn what it is and what to do about it. Learn all about greenwashing, including Futerra's ten signs of greenwashing.

Helfand, Judith, and Daniel Gold, producers. Blue Vinyl. http://www.bluevinyl.org/. "With a lighthearted tone, the film follows one woman's quest for an environmentally sound cladding for her parents' house in Merrick, Long Island, New York. It also investigates the many negative health effects of polyvinyl chloride in its production, use, and disposal, focusing on the communities of Lake Charles and Mossville, Louisiana, and Venice, Italy."

"It's Green—Find Out What It Really Means." Buildings. 2008. http://www.buildings.com/tabid/3334/ArticleID/5834/Default.aspx. "Learn the lingo (and what questions to ask) in order to make informed green-product purchases."

Part 260—Guides for the Use of Environmental Marketing Claims. http://www.ftc.gov/bcp/grnrule/guides980427.htm. These guides represent administrative interpretations of laws administered by the Federal Trade Commission for the guidance of the public in conducting its affairs in conformity with legal requirements. These guides specifically address the application of Section 5 of the FTC Act to environmental advertising and marketing practices.

"Sources of Indoor Air Pollution—Organic Gases." nebdoctors.com/download.php?f=Doc_8.pdf. Volatile organic chemicals (VOCs) are emitted as gases from certain solids or liquids. VOCs include a variety of chemicals, some of which may have short- and long-term adverse health effects.

What Makes a Building Material Green? Global Green U.S.A. http://globalgreen.org/competition/pdfs/03_green_material.pdf. Fostering a global value shift toward a sustainable and secure future.

Chapter Five

Indoor Environmental Quality

Let the clean air blow the cobwebs from your body. Air is medicine.—Lillian Russell (1862–1922)

The Earth's atmosphere contains three gases vital to plant life: oxygen, carbon dioxide, and nitrogen. These gases are exchanged or used internally by plants to transpire or make food. Air allows the sun's energy to heat the Earth and create weather, such as warmth and water, which is needed for plant life. Plants use carbon dioxide and give off oxygen. Animals, both human and otherwise, need fresh air for respiration and for transport of heat and vapor emitted from their bodies. Poor air quality negatively affects plants and animals alike.

Indoor environmental quality (IEQ), as stated by the Centers for Disease Control and Prevention (CDC), "simply refers to the quality of the air in an office or other building environments."[1] As the CDC points out, "Workers are often concerned that they have symptoms or health conditions from exposures to contaminants in the buildings where they work."[2] There is reason for this. People spend almost 90 percent of their time indoors. People who work in libraries and the patrons we serve are no exception. In fact, as a community center and a place of learning, there is perhaps a greater expectation that the atmosphere in the library will be clean and inviting.

When constructing cost-effective library buildings, it is important to realize that the success or failure of a project may rest on its indoor environmental quality. Healthy, comfortable library employees are more likely to be more satisfied and productive. Yet indoor environments are complex. If not monitored carefully while under construction and during operation, library staff members and patrons alike may be exposed to a variety of contaminants.

WHAT IS INDOOR ENVIRONMENTAL QUALITY?

Achieving good indoor environmental quality is more than avoiding contaminants. It also involves implementing ventilation strategies, cleaning the indoor air, and achieving physical comfort, which includes ergonomic, aesthetic, thermal, visual, and acoustical comfort.

There are many benefits to library staff and other occupants of a library building with good IEQ:

- Improved long-term health for current and future generations
- Decreased physical symptoms and associated health care costs
- Improved cognitive function
- Improved mood
- Increased productivity

Good IEQ in turn accrues to the library's bottom line:

- Reduced insurance and liability costs
- Decreased absenteeism and less substitute staffing
- Improved productivity
- Less turnover in staffing
- Improved community livability for library patrons
- Improved stakeholder relationships
- Improved profile with businesses and the pro-green community

The best way to achieve good IEQ is to use a whole-systems approach. You can facilitate quality IEQ through good design, construction, and operating and maintenance practices. Furthermore, every element of the library building can or should influence IEQ, and many of these elements, approached correctly, can also impact energy performance positively. Controlling IEQ, after all, is much more doable if you build source control into all the elements of design, construction, and operations.

SICK BUILDING SYNDROME AND BUILDING-RELATED ILLNESS

With all the time people spend indoors, the importance of indoor environmental quality cannot be overstated. While typically concerned, as we should be, with the outdoor air quality, designing optimum indoor environments and monitoring them are of utmost importance. In fact, IEQ was one of the first core issues in green building design, construction, and operation addressed as far back as the 1980s. A 1984 World Health Organization Committee report suggested that up to 30 percent of new and remodeled buildings worldwide may have been the subject of excessive complaints related to indoor air quality (IAQ).[3]

As outlined in that same report, the complaints can be put into two categories: sick building syndrome (SBS) or building-related illness (BRI). Indicators for SBS include these items:

- Headache
- Eye, nose, or throat irritation
- Dry cough
- Dry or itchy skin
- Dizziness and nausea
- Difficulty in concentrating; fatigue
- Sensitivity to odors
- The cause of the symptoms is not being known
- Relief of symptoms soon after leaving the building[4]

Indicators of BRI include these factors:

- Cough
- Chest tightness
- Fever, chills, and muscle aches
- Symptoms that are clinically defined and have clearly identifiable causes
- Prolonged recovery times after leaving the building[5]

The cost of sick buildings in the United States is staggering. For that reason, an increasing number of indoor air quality specialists in government agencies, academia, and the emerging industry are working to solve these problems. By some estimates, direct medical costs associated with IAQ problems in the United States are as high as $15 billion per year, with indirect costs of $60 billion. These estimates do not include problems like asthma, which may be triggered by IAQ problems—and which increased 42 percent between 1982 and 1992 in the United States, according to the latest statistics from the Centers for Disease Control.[6]

It is important to note that complaints may result from other causes. These may include an illness contracted from another source (e.g., human contact), acute sensitivity (e.g., allergies), job-related stress, or other psychosocial factors. With all these caveats, studies show that symptoms may be caused or exacerbated by indoor air quality problems.

There are three basic strategies to enhance indoor environmental quality. They are (1) source control and pathway interruption, (2) improved ventilation, and (3) air cleaners. Source control and pathway interruption relies on understanding the source of contaminants and pollutants and avoiding bringing them indoors and eliminating those that inevitably enter. Let us begin with a more complete look at the pollutants that you will need to guard against, pollutants identified as such by the EPA.[7]

GREEN MATERIALS

Green materials contribute to the overall environment. Rapidly renewables and recycled materials are gentler to the environment and may be appropriate when reflecting the library's sense of place. The materials used in the library building can also contribute positively to the indoor environment if green materials are chosen and installed. (See chapter 4, "Green Materials.") If green materials are not used, the reverse will most likely be true.

TEMPERATURE/HUMIDITY LEVELS

The University of California, San Diego, has developed guidelines for environmental (temperature and humidity) levels.[8] According to these guidelines, in the general stacks, the temperature should range from 68–72°F, and the relative humidity levels should range from 40 to 55 percent. Closed stacks temperatures should be kept at 60°F. Humidity levels for rare materials should be no more than 45 percent while films and music should be stored at 50 percent. These guidelines should be read carefully and followed closely.

POLLUTANTS

It's better to avoid pollutants and contaminants than to try to eliminate them once they have been introduced inside the library. What follows is a list of many of the most common pollutants that cause health and comfort problems.

Asbestos: No longer used in new construction, asbestos might be an issue if your library project includes a renovation or old building demolition. Asbestos, a cancer and lung disease hazard, is found in many older buildings but becomes hazardous when disturbed during renovation or demolition. The Occupational Safety and Health Administration (OSHA) developed standards to protect workers from exposure to asbestos in the workplace. 29 CFR 1926.1101 covers construction work, including alteration, repair, renovation, and demolition of structures containing asbestos.[9]

Biological pollutants: Also called low hazards, these are agents that do not cause disease but that decrease the aesthetic quality of the environment. These are in contrast to biological contaminants (high hazards) that cause disease.

Carbon monoxide (CO): Carbon monoxide is a deadly, colorless, odorless, poisonous gas. It is produced by the incomplete burning of various fuels, including coal, wood, charcoal, oil, kerosene, propane, and natural gas. Products and equipment powered by internal combustion engines such as portable generators, cars, lawn mowers, and power washers also produce CO.[10]

Formaldehyde/pressed wood products: All wood has trace amounts of formaldehyde naturally, which is why the focus is on added urea-formaldehyde (UF). By selecting natural woods or pressed wood products UF, you minimize exposure to this indoor air contaminant.

Lead (Pb): Lead has long been recognized as a harmful environmental pollutant. In 1991 the secretary of the Department of Health and Human Services called lead the "number one environmental threat to the health of children in the United States." Before it was known how harmful lead was, it was used in paint, gasoline, water pipes, and many other products. Old lead-based paint is the most significant source of lead exposure in the United States today. Harmful exposures can be created when lead-based paint is improperly removed from surfaces by dry scraping, sanding, or open-flame burning. High concentrations of airborne lead particles in homes can also result from lead dust from outdoor sources, including contaminated soil tracked inside, and use of lead in certain indoor activities such as soldering and stained-glass making. Airborne lead enters the body when an individual breathes or swallows lead particles or dust once it has settled.[11]

Nitrogen dioxide (NO_2): Nitrogen dioxide is a toxic gas that is a highly reactive oxidant and corrosive. The primary sources indoors are combustion processes, such as unvented combustion appliances (e.g., gas stoves), vented appliances with defective installations, welding, and tobacco smoke.[12]

Pesticides: According to the EPA, a pesticide is a chemical used to prevent, destroy, or repel pests. Pests can be insects, mice and other animals, weeds, fungi, or microorganisms such as bacteria and viruses. Some examples of pests are termites causing damage to our homes, dandelions in the lawn, and fleas on our dogs and cats. Pesticides also are used to kill organisms that can cause diseases.[13]

Radon: Radon (Rn) is the second leading cause of lung cancer in general and the first leading cause of lung cancer in nonsmokers. Radon is naturally occurring in the soil, formed by the decay of uranium or thorium. Radon is prevalent in some locales, absent in others. It can enter the library through cracks and openings in the floors and walls that come in contact with the ground. Radon does not occur evenly throughout the country. Some regions have more, some less. The EPA had developed a map that reflects radon zones.[14] Regardless of which zone your library is located, you should test for radon and mitigate if necessary. The commonly recommended action level for radon exposure is over 4 picocuries per liter or air (pCi/L).

If the area is tested and radon is present, mitigation should be included in your library building plan, whether building from the ground up or renovating. Mitigation can take a number of forms. Work with your design team to come up with the best solution.

Dangerous levels of radon may also occur in water, especially if it high levels are found in the air. Therefore it is best to test the air first. If radon levels in the air are high, and your water comes from a well (which is somewhat unlikely), it would be good to test the water too. Although no standard for unacceptable levels have been set, 300–400 picocuries per liter of water are being considered.[15] If your source of water is from a municipality, testing the water will not be necessary because municipalities test the water routinely. Radon in the water can also be mitigated.

Respirable particles: These are particles such as dust and mold that you may breathe in. Molds are living things that produce spores that float in the air, land on damp surfaces, and grow. Inhaling or touching molds can cause hay fever-type symptoms such as sneezing, runny nose, red eyes, skin rashes, and even asthma. To avoid molds, moisture levels should be no more than 55 percent. Sixty percent is the lower limit of microbial growth. As damaging as mold is for human health, it is also damaging for books and other library resource materials. Guard against excessive moisture to avoid damaging your collection. This is of particular concern if there is a rare book room or an archive.

Secondhand smoke/environmental tobacco smoke: Secondhand smoke comes from burning tobacco products. It can cause cancer and serious respiratory illnesses and is especially damaging to children. Indoor smoking in public spaces is illegal in most states, but it is important to clearly state that your library is a no-smoking space.

Stoves, heaters, fireplaces, and chimneys: Combustion pollutants are gases or particulates that come from improperly vented or unvented fuel-burning appliances such as space heaters, gas stoves, water heaters, dryers, and fireplaces. The types and amounts of pollutants produced depend on the type of appliance, how well the appliance is installed, maintained, and vented, and the kind of fuel it uses. Common combustion pollutants include carbon monoxide (CO), which is a colorless, odorless gas that interferes with the delivery of oxygen throughout the body. Carbon monoxide causes headaches, dizziness, weakness, nausea, and even death. Nitrogen dioxide (NO_2) is another colorless, odorless gas and causes eye, nose and throat irritation, shortness of breath, and an increased risk of respiratory infection.

Volatile organic compounds (VOCs): Volatile organic compounds are chemicals found in paints and lacquers, paint strippers, cleaning supplies, varnishes and waxes, pesticides, building materials and furnishings, office equipment, moth repellents, air fresheners, and dry-cleaned clothing. VOCs evaporate into the air when these products are used or sometimes even when they are stored. Volatile organic compounds irritate the eyes, nose, and throat and cause headaches, nausea, and damage to the liver, kidneys, and central nervous system. Several VOCs present in indoor air "have caused cancer in animal studies when the animals were exposed to high concentrations." A few VOCs, for example formaldehyde and benzene, are "considered by many authorities to be proven or probable human carcinogens."[16]

VENTILATION

The second strategy for good indoor environmental quality is good ventilation systems. Ventilation can control indoor humidity and airborne contaminants, both of which either contribute to or act as health hazards. The American Society of Heating, Refrigerating, and Air Conditioning Engineers (ASHRAE) and several states (e.g., Minnesota, Washington, and Vermont) have ventilation standards (ASHRAE Standard 62.1) designed to ensure enhanced indoor air quality with good HVACR systems, proper ventilation rates, and indoor air quality procedures. High indoor humidity can spur mold growth. High humidity may result from poor construction/rehabilitation, site design that does not properly manage water, and inadequate air exchange. A reasonable target for relative humidity is 30–60 percent. In cool climates, inadequate ventilation in the winter can contribute to excessive moisture and humidity because normal activities (e.g., breathing) create moisture, and there is insufficient natural ventilation (opening windows) or mechanical ventilation (fans, exhaust systems) to remove the moisture. In warmer climates, the heating, ventilation, and air conditioning (HVAC) system can pull warmer and humid air inside. In this case, the ventilation system may help create indoor humidity problems unless the system also dehumidifies the air. In any case it is important to understand air exchange rates.

Suffice it to say that the design, construction, and commissioning of the heating, ventilation, air conditioning, and refrigeration (HVACR) systems are complex and beyond the scope of this book. It is best to refer to the *Indoor Air Quality Guide: Best Practices for Design, Construction, and Commissioning*[17] for guidance on addressing IAQ during building design and construction. The *Indoor Air Quality Guide* was developed by an ASHRAE-appointed team of building professionals and world class IAQ experts with funding support from the EPA.

More specific information regarding the effects of IAQ on people's health and performance can be found by consulting *Indoor Air Quality Scientific Findings Resource Bank (IAQ-SFRB)* for information about the effects of IAQ on people's health or work performance. The IAQ-SFRB is being developed by the Indoor Environment Department of the Lawrence Berkeley National Laboratory with funding support from the United States.[18]

A library building with good indoor environmental quality is one that has an appropriate air exchange rate.[19] While this is not something that you, the librarian, need calculate, it is something to be aware of and ask your mechanical engineer or HVACR professional about. One such standard to be aware of is the *ASHRAE Standard: Ventilation for Acceptable Indoor Air Quality,* It includes minimum ventilation rates for various breathing zones, including libraries. Your professional will need to have estimates of occupancy, which you can furnish given staffing levels, and numbers of patrons at various times per day. Consider that your patron levels will increase when you have a new or newly renovated facility to enjoy.

Air flow inside the library is essential to the occupants' health because certain pollutants can reside inside, and, without proper airflow, these pollutants can cause serious health problems. According to the EPA, "Inadequate ventilation can increase indoor pollutant levels by not bringing in enough outdoor air to dilute emissions from indoor sources and by not carrying indoor air pollutants out of the home. High temperature and humidity levels can also increase concentrations of some pollutants."[20]

Adequate air exchange dilutes pollutants. As it is often said, "dilution is the solution to pollution." However, that is not the preferred strategy. It's better to avoid or eliminate the pollutants. One easy way is to use walk-off mats in the entryways to prevent dust and other contaminants from entering. Another technique is to monitor for pollutants. Particulates in the air, as well as moisture and humidity levels, can be monitored and measured. Air cleaners can be installed. CO_2 and CO monitors can help to determine if there are sufficient air exchanges for the library building's occupancy levels. Dust sampling can be done before and during a renovation to determine if there are any lead particulates in the air. Certainly this should also be done after construction is complete to be sure any lead had been mitigated.

Be sure to isolate the source when tracking or mitigating pollutants. That is, segregate and vent areas with either chemical or other concentrated odors, such as office equipment rooms, graphics areas, kitchens, and bathrooms. Moreover, it is important to position such vents away from any intake vents. These areas also need to be identified and planned for early in the design phase.

POLLUTANT MANAGEMENT DURING DEMOLITION AND CONSTRUCTION

High-efficiency filters are also an important part of good indoor air quality. Filters in the HVAC system and filters in your vacuum cleaner are equally important. Filters play a significant role in managing particulates, thus keeping allergens and irritants at bay. It is important to know that filters have MERV (minimum efficiency reporting value) ratings. Especially high-efficiency filters are needed during construction. LEED® has specified minimum MERV ratings both during construction and during operation. For the librarian it is important to know about MERV filters and that different circumstances call for different MERV ratings.

Avoiding pollutants does not consist solely of using green products and controlling pollutants after construction. Demolition projects and building construction pose unique challenges in pollution prevention. Demolition may cause the workers to come into contact with all sorts of pollutants, some of which are no longer allowable, including lead and asbestos. Removal of asbestos or lead should be done by certified professionals according to specific rules and regulations. Demolition and construction create dust that pollutes the air and creates health problems. There is need for a dust control plan that covers disturbances during the project, from site preparation to building completion. Be aware of jurisdictional requirements regarding particulate matter and fugitive dust. Besides health concerns, significant dust disturbances can lead to citations and fines. Since each project is different, generating its own unique combination of wastes and pollutants, the project manager must be flexible and creative in finding ways to reduce or eliminate human exposure to the pollutants and filter them or dispose of them in an environmentally responsible way.

When reviewing your IEQ construction management plan, be sure that one of two alternatives regarding the library's HVAC air handler is included. Do not use the air handler while construction is in progress, or, if the HVAC is used during construction, use MERV-8 filters in the system. Also implement the 2007 (or later) Sheet Metal and Air Conditioning Contractors' National Association (SMACNA) IAQ guidelines. These guidelines include ways to protect the HVAC, source control, pathway interruption, scheduling the construction to limit exposure to dust, and housekeeping (e.g., regular sweeping and vacuuming).

GREEN CLEANING

After building or renovating your library with its enhanced indoor air quality, you want to keep it that way. According to the Ashkin Group, each year, 6 billion pounds of chemicals and 4.5 billion pounds of paper products (representing about 25 to 50 million trees) are used to clean commercial buildings.[21] Rather than add to those numbers, it would be better to procure green products for cleaning as an essential strategy for keeping good air quality. Although you may not need many new products right away, you will need cleaning supplies. Cleaning products that your library may have used in the past may contain harmful chemicals that can have serious adverse effects on the library's janitorial staff, building occupants, and the environment. Library personnel handling cleaning products used to clean floors, carpets, plumbing fixtures, and other building elements can be at risk for a number of adverse health effects. Janitorial products can cause harm to the environment during their use if they are poured down the drain, circulated through the library's ventilation systems, or disposed of outdoors. Environmental damage can also occur during the development, manufacture, and transport of these products. Possible environmental consequences of janitorial products include

- Air pollution
- Bioaccumulation of toxic substances in plants and animals
- Endocrine disruption in wildlife, which affects reproductive ability
- Ozone depletion[22]

THERMAL, ERGONOMIC, VISUAL, AND ACOUSTICAL COMFORT

As important as good air quality is to occupant comfort and good health, there are other considerations that affect not only occupant comfort and productivity but also energy efficiency and operations. The library project team also needs to consider and plan for the occupants' thermal, ergonomic, visual, and acoustical comfort.

There are six factors to consider when evaluating the conditions for optimal thermal comfort:

- Air temperature
- Relative humidity
- Surface temperatures that influence radiation
- Occupants' personal metabolic rates
- Amount of clothing worn by occupants
- Air speed across body surfaces[23]

Ergonomics is the application of scientific information to the design of objects, systems, and environments for human use. It incorporates elements from many subjects including anatomy, physiology, psychology, and design. Environmental ergonomics applies its diverse knowledge base to products and environments to ensure that they are comfortable, safe, and efficient for people to use. Be sure that your interior designer is familiar with and applies the principles of environmental ergonomics as the interior space is designed and the furniture is selected.

Designing the work environment ergonomically—that is, to meet the needs of the user—is critical to the overall success of the project, as the Air

Force has concluded. Specific goals for the library's indoor environmental quality might well include those established by the Air Force:

- Decrease the occurrence and cost of accidents, injuries, and disabilities
- Improve the well-being and readiness of the organization
- Optimize the performance of organizational systems
- Decrease physical and cognitive stress on personnel
- Increase job satisfaction and productivity[24]

Visual comfort is part aesthetic and part practical. Achieving visual comfort includes creating visually interesting environments and using effective artificial lighting and daylighting. It may also include what people see out the windows, what colors are used inside and out, and how the building is designed both inside and out. Where are your tall stacks? Will they block your daylighting plans? Are there windows for staff offices? How do windows in staff offices affect the number and surface area of windows in the public part of the library? Will skylights be helpful in achieving the daylighting that is desired?

Visual comfort is also an essential element in the library's sense of place, as first discussed in chapter 2, "The Importance of Place." Your design team needs to ask itself a series of questions when considering design. The answers to these and similar questions will be what heighten the library's visual interest and its sense of place:

- What is your library's mission? How might your library's values and culture be expressed physically in your building?
- What will your library's façade, entrance, and reception area look like? What will its look express? Will the design draw your community in?
- How can your library showcase your community's culture, its artifacts, and its local ecology? What local materials, artisans, and designs can be featured?
- How will the local environment be reflected in your library? Consider that the desert Southwest is a very different place from verdant Northwest. The library needs to reflect those regional differences by the use of daylight, views, design motifs, and natural materials.
- How will you use color in your library's surfaces, furnishings, and artifacts? Often institutions use grays and beiges, shying away from color. The library needs to use color effectively to uplift and inspire. Color can also distinguish one area from another. Signage, often coordinated to the area color, can also be used to differentiate one area from another.
- How might you provide both library users and staff with daylight? Natural, full-spectrum light is a human biological need. Daylight stimulates the human visual and circadian system. Daylight, which varies at different

times during different seasons and in different regions, will need to be considered. Although lighting technology continues to improve, daylighting is preferred. The specifics of daylighting are covered in chapter 3, "Energy and Lighting."

Art is also something to think about when considering visual comfort. Paul Shrivastava contends that combining arts with science will help to bring about the passionate implementation of sustainable development: "No significant human endeavour has ever been accomplished without passion. Science and technology by themselves aren't enough. We need to turn to the arts in order to infuse passion into the pursuit of sustainability and get real results that will heal the planet."[25] He argues that art is a survival instinct. "Narratives, stories, music and images served to warn our early ancestors against predators and natural disasters. Art helped them develop defence mechanisms. My colleagues and I believe that art should be used to deal with modern survival threats such as climate change and environmental crises."[26] Art will make the library a more visually pleasing place to work or play and demonstrate to the people who are employed and people you serve that a sustainable library and sustainable architecture has an important purpose. As Shrivastava states hopefully: "We've spent decades relying on science and technology and the planet is still in shambles. Art allows fresh perspectives and new ways interpreting the world. . . . Art is what will make us give up our old habits in favour of planet-changing behaviour."[27] What better place to change behavior so crucial to the planet's survival than in a library?

Acoustical comfort is also a key consideration. It is important to determine what might be background noises, what sounds might be reflected or absorbed, what the acoustical qualities of your spaces are, and how sound might transfer from one space to another. Certainly quiet spaces are of utmost importance in your library. Spaces for reading. Spaces for study and learning. Spaces for quiet contemplation. Spaces where important work can be done. Spaces for private conversations. Equally important are the spaces where sound will happen naturally and appropriately. Spaces for group meetings. Spaces for staff interaction. Spaces for presentations and performances. Spaces for teaching. Spaces for conferencing. It is important to design these spaces discretely so that sound from these areas does not bleed into the quiet spaces. All of this while building flexibility into your design.

Many industry standards deal with noise reduction coefficiency and reverberation rates. These standards for minimum acoustical performance include: *American National Standards Institute/ASHRAE Standard S12.60-2002*[28] (for classrooms), the *ASHRAE Handbook,* Chapter 47, "Sound and Vibration Control," *2003 HVAC Applications Handbook,* and American Society of Interior Designer's *Sound Solutions.*[29]

System analysis for noise control uses the source-path-receiver concept. The source of the sound is the noise-generating mechanism. The sound travels from the source via a path, which can be through the air (airborne) or through the structure (structureborne), or a combination of both paths, until it reaches the receiver (building occupant or outdoor neighbor).

INDIVIDUAL COMFORT

When it comes down to it, physical comfort (thermal, ergonomic, visual, acoustical) is individual. There are no absolutes. Therefore it is best to build in as many opportunities as possible for the individual to regulate (within reason) their own environment, including lighting, ventilation, and temperature (individual thermostats, windows that open, etc.). For instance, it is best for windows to open. But with windows that open, you need to figure out a way for individuals to determine whether or not the air conditioning is on so that they will close the windows when it is. Lighting might be connected to motion detectors, but only if there is sufficient movement in the room so that lights stay on when people are stationary at their computers. When possible, consider installing full spectrum lighting that mimics daylighting. It portrays true colors; reduces glare, fatigue, and eye strain; illuminates details and color; makes work environments more productive; and brings the benefits and beauty of the outdoors to a library's interior space.

COMMISSIONING

ASHRAE Guideline 0, the Commissioning Process, defines commissioning as "a quality-oriented process for achieving, verifying, and documenting that the performance of facilities, systems, and assemblies meets defined objectives and criteria."[30]

Commissioning (Cx) is, in fact, a process by which you can assure that a building performs in accordance with the design intent and the owner's operational needs. According to the Building Commissioning Association (BCA), "Building commissioning provides documented confirmation that building systems function according to criteria." No matter how well you design the building, no matter how careful the contractor, engineers, and others on the design team execute their responsibilities, there is bound to be something that did not happen exactly right. Commissioning before the building is occupied is one way to detect those things that are not working properly and fixing them before move-in. Enhanced commissioning is better still. This entails recommissioning the library after a year or so of operation. By that time, problems might have been detected that were not detected immediately after the building was substantially completed, and it allows a chance to diagnose problems that might otherwise go unanswered and lead people to believe that sustainable buildings are not as environmentally sound as might have been advertised. Enhanced commissioning requires that the building operate within the parameters of a written systems manual available for use in the process. A written systems manual is important with or without enhanced commissioning. It is important that your staff know how to operate the systems that the contractor installs. Without a systems manual, systems will not run as efficiently as they might and economic savings and personal comfort may not be realized to the fullest extent possible. If you decide on enhanced commissioning to meet LEED credit, please be sure to read and follow all criteria around achieving this credit. Commissioning is best done by a third-party, certificated commissioning professional. In fact, this is required by LEED and some government entities. However, commissioning can also be done by the owner, architect, contractor, etc. For more information regarding commissioning, see chapter 8, "Building Operations and Maintenance."

POST-OCCUPANCY SURVEYS

Post-occupancy surveys are one method of evaluating user satisfaction. As Christopher N. Henry stated, "They can be very useful and should be implemented as long as architects do not expect or claim too much from them.[31] These surveys, however, can be used to benchmark a building's performance against others or benchmark your library against itself. Administered soon after occupancy, the survey can be a diagnostic tool that serves to expose occupant dissatisfaction and detailed information, if asked, regarding the nature of the problems. Once the problems are addressed, the survey can be repeated to assess the effectiveness of the solutions applied. Sample surveys are available in the literature.[32]

RELEVANT CODES AND STANDARDS FOR IEQ

These guidelines and standards are listed in the Whole Building Design Guide's *Enhance Indoor Environmental Quality (IEQ)*. This IEQ overview is well done and well worth reading in its entirety.[33]

- *ASHRAE Guideline 1.1-2007: HVAC&R Technical Requirements for the Commissioning Process*
- *ASHRAE Standards 52.2: Method of Testing General Ventilation Air-Cleaning Devices for Removal Efficiency by Particle Size*
- *ASHRAE Standard 62.1: Ventilation for Acceptable Indoor Air Quality*
- *ASHRAE Standard 90.1: Energy Standard for Buildings Except Low-Rise Residential Buildings*

- *ASHRAE 189.1-2011: Standard for the Design of Green Buildings Except Low-Rise Residential Buildings*
- *Air Force Engineering Technical Letter ETL 04-3: Design Criteria for Prevention of Mold in Air Force Facilities*
- *P100 Facilities Standards for the Public Buildings Service*

EXAMPLES

Multnomah County Library's Hillsdale Library won LEED Gold in 2004. One of the reasons for the award was its enhanced indoor air quality. According to the library website:

- Smoking is not allowed inside the library, or within 50 feet of the entry.
- The building is monitored for carbon dioxide levels and is designed to maintain levels that will sustain long-term occupant health and comfort.
- Fresh air is mixed into the mechanical system to support the health, safety, and comfort of people in the building.
- Filters within the mechanical system were used during construction to prevent contamination from the construction process. The building was "flushed" prior to opening to the public. This process involved running the mechanical system for two weeks following the completion of construction, and bringing 100 percent fresh air into the building. All filters were then replaced to remove construction-related contaminants from the system.
- All paint on the walls and steel structure, as well as all adhesives and sealants, are low VOC (volatile organic compounds), containing little or none of the dangerous chemicals commonly found in these materials.
- "Walk-off" mats in entryways help prevent pollutants from being tracked into the library.
- Storage for chemical products, such as cleaning supplies and printing products, is contained in isolated or ventilated rooms.
- Temperature is controlled and monitored with the use of sensors throughout the building.
- Windows, clerestory and skylights enhance the connection between indoor and outdoor environments, providing natural outdoor light and offering library visitors great views of the neighborhood. In addition, a manual shading system allows control over direct sunlight and helps reduce heat gain.[34]

University of California, Santa Cruz, Science and Engineering Library Lighting Upgrade is listed as one of the 2011 Best Practices case studies which were coordinated by the Green Building Research Center at the University of California, Berkeley.

An in-house project team at UC Santa Cruz used data-logging tools and lighting simulation software to identify and test cost-effective energy-saving strategies. Once implemented these strategies yielded savings of 52 percent.

The retrofitted reduced lighting fixture counts and illumination levels saved energy while also enhancing visual comfort for library users."[35]

YOUR PROJECT NOTES

1. Do the examples put forth give you any ideas that you might want to use in your library project?

2. What is your library's mission? How might your library's values and culture be expressed physically? What role might art play in this expression?

3. What is your layout and how will it take advantage of daylighting? Where will your tall shelving be placed? Where are your banks of computers located? Have you made the best use of any daylighting that your library building might afford? To whom? Staff? Patrons?

4. What type of heating system will you install in your library? Why? What kind of comfort will it provide staff and patrons? How will comfort balance with the costs of operation?

5. Do you want to specify that the contractor must provide you with a complete systems operations manual? Does that need to be specified in the original request for proposal?

6. Do you have a plan for green cleaning for your library once the building is complete and the library is open to the public?

NOTES

1. Centers for Disease Control and Prevention (CDC), "Workplace Safety and Health Tips," http://www.cdc.gov/niosh/topics/indoorenv/.
2. CDC, "Workplace Safety and Health Tips."
3. Environmental Protection Agency (EPA), "Indoor Air Facts No. 4 Sick Building Syndrome, Revised," http://www.epa.gov/iaq/pdfs/sick_building_factsheet.pdf.
4. EPA, "Indoor Air Facts."
5. EPA, "Indoor Air Facts."
6. "The IAQ Challenge: Protecting the Indoor Environment," *Environmental Building News*, May 1, 1996, http://www.buildinggreen.com/auth/article.cfm/1996/5/1/The-IAQ-Challenge-Protecting-the-Indoor-Environment/.
7. EPA, "Indoor Air: An Introduction to Indoor Air Quality (IAQ), Biological Pollutants," http://www.epa.gov/iaq/biologic.html.
8. For more information regarding temperature and humidity levels for libraries, see "Temperature/Humidity Levels for UCSD Libraries," http://libraries.ucsd.edu/preservation/collectionprespolicytempRH.html.
9. OSHA Fact Sheet: AsbestosFacts, http://www.osha.gov/OshDoc/data_AsbestosFacts/asbestos-factsheet.pdf.
10. U.S. Consumer Product Safety Commission, "Carbon Monoxide Questions and Answers," http://www.cpsc.gov/cpscpub/pubs/466.html.
11. EPA, "An Introduction to Indoor Air Quality (IAQ): Lead (BP)," http://www.epa.gov/iaq/lead.html.
12. EPA, "An Introduction to Indoor Air Quality (IAQ)," http://www.epa.gov/iaq/no2.html#Health_Effects.
13. EPA, "What Is a Pesticide?," http://www.epa.gov/kidshometour/pest.htm.
14. EPA, "EPA Map of Radon Zones," http://www.epa.gov/radon/zonemap.html.
15. U.S. Inspect, "Radon in Water Q&A," http://www.usinspect.com/resources-for-you/advisory-report-archives/2003-archives/radon-water-q.
16. Lawrence Berkeley National Laboratory, "Indoor Air Quality Scientific Findings Resource Bank: Indoor Volatile Organic Compounds (VOCs) and Health, Cancer," 2013, http://www.iaqscience.lbl.gov/voc-cancer.html.
17. For more information regarding the *Indoor Air Quality Guide: The Best Practices for Design, Construction and Commissioning*, see http://www.techstreet.com/cgi-bin/detail?product_id=1703605.
18. *Enhance Indoor Environmental Quality*, Whole Building Design Guide, http://www.wbdg.org/design/ieq.php.
19. Paul Mesler," http://www.ehow.com/how_7242261_calculate-air-exchange.html#ixzz28Cx1XgSQ.
20. EPA, "An Introduction to Indoor Air Quality (IAQ): Lead (BP)."
21. Ashkin Group, "What Green Cleaning Can Mean to You," ashkingroup.com/PowerPoint/BSCAI%203-25-04_drh.pps.

22. Green Cleaning Pollution Prevention Calculator, http://www.fedcenter.gov/index.cfm?id=5432.

23. "Indoor Environmental Quality," Certainteed.com, http://www.certainteed.com/BuildingScience/Indoor-Environmental-Quality.

24. Air Force Center for Engineering and the Environment, "Ergonomics in the Work Environment," http://www.wbdg.org/0D16CE2C-C52C-43E6-ABDD-04737C037B9E/FinalDownload/DownloadId-156287228C675D7E66346AA1FA6C72F1/0D16CE2C-C52C-43E6-ABDD-04737C037B9E/ccb/AF/AFDG/interiordesign.pdf .

25. "The Art of Sustainable Development," *Science Daily*, October 19, 2012 http://www.sciencedaily.com/releases/2012/10/121019130606.htm#.UIaBfO4XjTs.email.

26. "The Art of Sustainable Development."

27. "The Art of Sustainable Development."

28. ANSI/ASA S12.60-2002, http://www.trane.com/commercial/library/vol32_1/index.asp#ansi.

29. American Society of Interior Designers, "Sound Solutions," http://www.ccrllc.com/Articles/ASIDSound.pdf.

30. "ASHRAE Guidelines: The Commissioning Process," ASHRAE, http://www.wbdg.org/project/buildingcomm.php.

31. Henry, Christopher N. "Post-Occupancy Surveys: Don't Ask Too Much from Them," *ArchDaily*, April 11, 2012, http://www.archdaily.com/225083/post-occupancy-surveys-dont-ask-too-much-from-them/.

32. For instance, see Leah Zagreus et al., *Listening to the Occupants: A Web-Based Indoor Environmental Quality Survey,* Wiley OnlineLibrary, http://www.cbe.berkeley.edu/research/pdf_files/Zagreus_2004_InAirSupp.pdf.

33. *Enhance Indoor Environmental Quality (IEQ),* Whole Building Design Guide, September 10, 2012, http://www.wbdg.org/design/ieq.php.

34. Multnomah County Library, "Leadership in Energy and Environmental Design," http://www.multcolib.org/agcy/hls-leed.html.

35. University of California Berkeley, Green Building Research Center, "UCSC Science & Engineering Library Lighting Upgrade: Best Practices Case Studies, 2011," http://greenbuildings.berkeley.edu/pdfs/bp2011-lighting-ucsc.pdf.

RESOURCES

Department of Health and Human Services, National Toxicology Program. *Report on Carcinogens.* 12th ed. http://ntp.niehs.nih.gov/ntp/roc/twelfth/roc12.pdf. The *Report on Carcinogens* (RoC) is an informational scientific and public health document that identifies and discusses agents, substances, mixtures, or exposure circumstances that may pose a hazard to human health by virtue of their carcinogenicity.

Environmental Protection Agency. "Building Radon Out." http://www.epa.gov/radon/pdfs/buildradonout.pdf. Although written for homes, the principles are sound and worth your understanding.

Gilbert, Steven G. "Public Health and the Precautionary Principle." *Northwest Public Health* Spring/Summer (2005): 4. The author's premise is that humanity has "the knowledge and resources to make appropriate decisions to protect the public health and the environment. The precautionary principle supports an approach to policy making that emphasizes our responsibility to future generations as we work together to manage the Commons."

Gilbert, Steven G. *A Small Dose of Toxicology: The Health Effects of Common Chemicals*, 2nd ed. Seattle: HWP, Healthy World Press, 2012. An introductory textbook on toxicology that examines the effects of common chemicals on our everyday lives.

Heerwagen, Judith H. *The Psychological Value of Space.* Whole Building Design Guide.http://www.wbdg.org/resources/psychspace_value.php. A prolific contributor to the field, Heerwagen contributes many works in this area that are oft-cited and well-respected.

Promote Health and Well-Being. Whole Building Design Guide. http://www.wbdg.org/design/promote_health.php. Various attributes of the indoor environment affect the occupants' health and well-being.

Ries, Robert, et al. "Economic Benefits of Green Buildings." *Engineering Economist,* September 22, 2006. http://www.highbeam.com/doc/1G1-152374315.html.

Woodstock Institute. "Nanotechnology Can Make Green Buildings Even Greener." September 26, 2007. http://www.wicnet.org/news/story.asp?id=210. Nanotechnologies help make buildings more sustainable and more cost-efficient.

Chapter Six

Water Conservation and Quality

Water is life's mater and matrix, mother and medium. There is no life without water.—Albert Szent-Gyorgyi (Hungarian Biochemist, 1937 Nobel Prize for Medicine, 1893–1986)

WHAT IS WATER?

Water, the most abundant liquid on Earth, is life's "mater and matrix." We drink it, we wash with it, we play in it, and we cook with it. In fact, our bodies are more than half water. It is impossible to overstate the importance of water to almost every process on Earth, from the life processes of the lowest life forms to the shaping of continents. Water is the most familiar chemical compound known to humans. Water allows life to exist on Earth. "A human may live a month with food, but only a week without water."[1]

Pure water is a colorless, odorless, tasteless substance made up of molecules containing one oxygen (O) atom and two hydrogen (H) atoms, which is why it is sometimes referred to as H_2O. Its physical and chemical properties allow you to freeze it, melt it, heat it, evaporate it, and combine it. Water can exist as a liquid, solid (ice), and gas (vapor). Liquid water becomes ice at 32°F and become vapor or steam at 202°F.

The Earth's supply of water is constantly being recycled. Called the hydrological cycle, water circulates continuously throughout Earth and between Earth's systems. At various stages, water, which in most cases is synonymous with the hydrosphere, moves through the atmosphere, the biosphere, and the geosphere. In each case it performs functions essential to the survival of the planet and its life forms. Thus, over time, water evaporates from the oceans; then falls as precipitation; is absorbed by the land; and, after some period of time, makes its way back to the oceans to begin the cycle again. The total amount of water on Earth may not have changed in many billions of years, though the distribution of water has.[2]

WATER, WATER EVERYWHERE

Everyone has heard the phrase, "Water, water everywhere and not a drop to drink," a paraphrased line from the *Rime of the Ancient Mariner*. Samuel Taylor Coleridge was right in the context of his poem and more broadly in the context of our planet because water covers about 70 percent of the Earth's surface. Water, including the clouds, makes our entire planet look blue and white from space. Yes, it's almost everywhere. However, 97% of the water on the Earth is salt water, and that was the water available to the sailors on the Mariner's ship. As the sailors understood, salt water is filled with salt and other minerals, and humans and other living creatures cannot drink this water. Although in the twenty-first century salt can be removed from the water, it is a difficult and expensive process.

Three percent of the Earth's water is fresh water. However, 2 percent of the water on Earth is glacier ice at the North and South Poles. This ice is fresh water and could be melted; however, it is too far away from where people live to be usable. That leaves less than 1 percent (or about 0.007 percent of all water on Earth) for human and animal use. We humans use this small amount of fresh water for drinking, transportation, heating and cooling, industry, and many other purposes. In fact, water is essential not only to personal health but also to healthy economic, geopolitical, and environmental conditions around the world. Yet due to population growth, climate change, and mismanagement, having adequate, affordable drinking and irrigation water is a growing international crisis.

Here are several sets of facts that bear this out: According to Population Action International, based upon the UN Medium Population Projections of 1998, more than 2.8 billion people in 48 countries will face water stress or scarcity conditions by 2025. Of these countries, 40 are in West Asia, North Africa, or sub-Saharan Africa. Over the next two decades, population increases and growing demands are projected to push all the West Asian countries into water scarcity conditions. By 2050, the number of countries facing water stress or scarcity could rise to 54, with a combined population of 4 billion people—about 40 percent of the projected global population of 9.4 billion.[3]

Not all shortages are elsewhere in other countries. Here in the United States there are looming shortages too:

> More than 1 in 3 counties in the United States could face a "high" or "extreme" risk of water shortages due to climate change by the middle of the twenty-first century, according to a new study in the American Chemical

Society's (ACS) journal *Environmental Science & Technology*. The new report concluded that 7 in 10 of the more than 3,100 U.S. counties could face "some" risk of shortages of fresh water for drinking, farming, and other uses. [4]

The numbers are staggering and frightening. The World Health Organization is working to secure clean water worldwide. It will be an uphill climb. About 1 billion people currently lack access to clean drinking water, and waterborne illnesses kill over 2 million people each year. More than 50 countries still report cholera to the World Health Organization. [5]

Shortages both here and globally will prompt shifting demographics. Areas of drought will be abandoned, and population will move to the remaining places where fresh water still exists. Water has already been dubbed *blue gold,* and people who move to places that have water have been termed "water refugees." Water rights have become precious commodities no longer taken for granted. Rights to water are established by actual use of the water and maintained by continued use and need. Water rights are treated similarly to rights to real property, can be conveyed, mortgaged, and encumbered in the same manner, all independently of the land on which the water originates or on which it is used. States now have laws on the books to handle disputes that are arising with increasing frequency.

With that in mind, it is important to understand the water resources in your own area and those specific to your library's site. Critical to that understanding is identifying your region's water resources, including watersheds, precipitation, areas of land that drain rainwater, aquifers, melting snow, and basins of streams, lakes, and rivers.

WATER CHALLENGES

In the United States and around the world, a number of water challenges face us. Humans have disrupted the natural hydrological cycle by population growth, pollution, building, infrastructure, irrigation, deforestation, and climate change. These factors have resulted in a smaller supply of fresh water, degraded water quality, and loss of habitat for wildlife. All these elements put pressure on water supplies and other resources. Water demand, water quality, and habitat protection will make new water sources difficult to find and consequently more expensive. The days of considering water as a free, inexhaustible resource have passed. Scarcity has entered into the conversation and potable water has become its own market. A 1998 Johns Hopkins study reported that the water industry had annual revenues estimated at $300 billion, and the United States was responsible for more than half of that amount. The study estimated that, using current water management, 35 percent of the global population will not have access to fresh water within twenty-five years. As Clay Landry and Terry Anderson observe, "With the impending water shortages countries are looking for new, innovative ways to manage this valuable resource."[6]

WATER USE DEFINITIONS

Water is used and reused. In determining the best strategies for your library building, both inside and out, it is necessary to understand the sources and types of water so better to match the source and type to the use:

- Potable: safe to drink; drinkable
- Rainwater: roof runoff or clean sort runoff
- Greywater: used water from sinks, laundry, and showers
- Blackwater: used water from toilets
- Combined water: greywater and blackwater
- Reclaimed water: water treated and sold for reuse by wastewater treatment plants
- Stormwater: water that originates from precipitation events that runs off surfaces such as rooftops, paved streets, highways, parking lots, and other impervious surfaces

OVERVIEW OF SUSTAINABLE WATER APPROACHES

The forecasts of a smaller supply of fresh water, degraded water quality, and loss of habitat for wildlife give us a glimpse of a future we don't want either for our library, our region, or our world. A number of questions need to be asked and answered in order to avoid that bleak future:

1. How can we deliver best-practice information in order to ensure that people (individually and in their homes) practice sustainable water use? What role can libraries play in demonstrating best practices regarding water use?
2. What best practices do cities and other jurisdictions need to adopt to secure the water supply in the face of climate change? What role can libraries play in educating your communities about these best practices that have been or may need to be adopted?
3. What changes are needed to the built environment and infrastructure to adapt to the effects of climate change? To the extent allowable in particular communities, what is the library's role?
4. What are the best practices in water demand management, including water efficiency, recycling, and integrated water management approaches? What best practices can libraries implement in order to respond to water scarcity and unreliable supply?

On what can best practices in water conservation be based? The answer lies in nature. First referred to in chapter 1, "The Fundamentals of Sustainable Building," biomimicry is the new science that studies nature's models and uses her designs and processes to solve human problems. Applying biomimicry to water conservation, the solutions will mimic nature, matching the water source to an appropriate use. For instance, potable water need not be used for irrigation or toilet flushing. Greywater would be appropriate for both such uses, saving potable water for consumption. Appropriate use is dictated by two conditions, the level of treatment needed for safe use, if any, and the regulatory barriers that exist locally. It is important that your team understand both conditions early in the design process. Observing nature, you can see that everything is recycled and renewed endlessly. In an effort to return, restore, and regenerate, it is important to use the land and landscape as gently as possible. And, as a library—an educational institution—it is important to return, restore, and regenerate. And, at the very least, reduce, reuse, and recycle.

As noted in chapter 2, "The Importance of Place," it is important to build your library with as little disturbance to the land as possible, conserving and protecting native vegetation and soil. It is also important to restore and regenerate the landscape by avoiding damage and returning the land, as much as is possible, to its natural habitat. Moving toward greater sustainability and stability, consider strategies such as wetlands, restoration of soils and site nutrients, bioswales, habitat corridors, and native plants and trees. As you consider these strategies, design with the library site's elements in mind, such as sun, shade, drainage, wind, temperature, precipitation, and other items discovered during the site visit and analysis. Make the landscape surrounding your library a pleasant place that is reflective of the area's native environment.

In addition, when building, it is essential to restore and enhance the building site and implement water efficiencies both inside and out. These are principles that libraries can adopt. In addition, the library can assume an educational role, educating the community regarding the need to conserve water and use it appropriately.

INDOOR WATER USE

These principles can be applied both indoors and out. Inside water conservation for your library begins with efficient equipment and fixtures for bathrooms, kitchenettes, staff areas, staff rooms, and janitors' closets. Fixtures and equipment tend to be low-cost with quick payback periods. The design team needs to research the fixtures for their pros and cons, typical costs, and major brands. There are many selection tools available, several of which are included in the Resources section at the end of the chapter (e.g., WaterSense and WaterWiser). Quality parts and fixtures are not only important to lower the amount of water used when the fixtures are functioning but also to prevent water leaks (e.g., dripping faucets and running toilets) when the water is supposed to be shut off.

Library Staff Room and Work Room Equipment: Dishwasher and Faucets

According to the EPA, if all households in the United States installed water-efficient appliances, the country would save more than 3 trillion gallons of water and more than $18 billion per year. The dishwasher in a staff room is not in a household and thus not included in this statistic. However, the statistic makes the point clear. It is imperative to purchase efficient, water-saving appliances. Energy Star models save water and energy. The average Energy Star dishwashers save 20 percent water. The tags on the appliances tell you how much. Once installed, scrape your dishes, don't rinse. Turn it on only when it's full. Use the ecowash cycle. To save energy, do not use the hot dry cycle.

Faucets account for more than 15 percent of indoor household water use—more than 1 trillion gallons of water across the United States each year. Again, this is a statistic that applies to households, but whether household or library, it indicates that leaky faucets are an issue. Be sure to fix a leaky kitchen faucet immediately; gallons of water can be wasted daily from what appears to be a minor leak. The aerator—the screw-on tip of the faucet—ultimately determines the maximum flow rate of a faucet. Make sure that the aerator is an efficient one. National standards dictate that pre-rinse spray valves use 1.6 gallons per minute at most.[7]

If for whatever reason you need to install a clothes washer and dryer in your library, again, check out the Energy Star models. A full-sized Energy Star certified clothes washer uses 15 gallons of water per load, compared to the 23 gallons used by a standard machine. Over the machine's lifetime, that's a savings of 2,500 gallons of water.[8]

Restrooms: Toilets, Urinals, and Showers

The bathroom is the largest consumer of indoor water. In a home the toilet alone can use 27 percent of household water. In a busy library, as a percentage of the whole, doubtlessly the toilets use an even great percentage of all the water used. Almost every activity or daily routine that happens in a bathroom uses a large quantity of water. WaterSense quotes these statistics:

- Older toilets use between 3.5 and 7 gallons of water per flush. However, WaterSense-labeled toilets require 75 to 80 percent less water.
- A leaky toilet, or one that is running constantly, can waste about 200 gallons of water every day.
- A bathroom faucet generally runs at 2 gallons of water per minute. [9]

Certain low-flush tank toilets do not operate well. To avoid problems, like not enough water to provide conveyance to the sewer system, careful selection is required especially when there are long sewer line runs or the drain slope is not steep enough. Maximum Performance (MaP) standards have been developed for all commercially available toilets. [10]

WaterSense estimates that nearly 65 percent of the urinals in use today exceed the maximum allowable flush volume set by federal standards. The current standard for commercial urinals is 1.0 gallon per flush (gpf). Some older urinals use as much as five times that amount. [11] Replacing these inefficient fixtures with WaterSense-labeled flushing urinals can save between 1.0 and 4.5 gallons per flush, without sacrificing performance. Installing Water-Sense-labeled flushing urinals will save money on water bills and preserve water resources.

Janitors' Closets

The specifications for the janitors' closets are mostly written to address indoor environmental quality. However, you should remember to equip each closet with a mop sink, hose and reel, and hot and cold drains.

SUSTAINABILITY PRICING

In places where water has been acknowledged as an increasingly scarce resource, sustainability pricing has been adopted. That is, some cities and other jurisdictions have begun to price water in a way that begins to reflect its true value. Water will no longer be an inexpensive commodity. So adopting water-saving tools and measures will not only help the environment, but it will also help the library's bottom line.

The recognition of the value of water and its scarcity has had an effect on our thinking. As our rivers run dry, our drying lakes shrink, and parts of our country suffer with drought, people have begun to ask questions like "Why are we using potable water to flush toilets? Why are we using potable water to irrigate our landscape and gardens? How can we make better use of the water we have?" One answer is the use of greywater and purple pipe. More and more municipalities are approving the use of properly designed greywater systems that allow water from bathroom sinks, showers, bathtubs, and clothes washers to be safely reused for watering and irrigation of gardens and landscapes and flush toilets. The greywater is separated from potable water, traveling through the building in purple pipe. This is not a solution that is available everywhere yet, but it is coming. Even if greywater use is not yet approved in your location, you might consider installing purple pipe so that you can use greywater when that becomes a possibility.

OUTSIDE WATER MANAGEMENT AND USE

The first step in outside water management is to be aware of the site's natural composition, including the natural water, drainage, wildlife, and vegetation, so as to sustain or regenerate the landscape wherever possible. But there are also a host of strategies in the built environment that can be employed to ease or negate the library building's impact on the land. Stormwater management is one of them. As more building and infrastructure covers the landscape, the land is less able to handle stormwater, especially at time of peak runoff. This result, if not mitigated, is erosion, water quality degradation, wildlife extinction, and overtaxed stormwater infrastructure.

Stormwater Management

Conventional stormwater management focuses primarily in accommodating the runoff but does not seek to find ways to minimize or eliminate it. Stormwater runs through a series of buried pipes and fenced detention ponds combining with the sewage system. In response to more and more development, the stormwater management infrastructure needs to grow at great expense to municipalities and thus to the taxpayers. If the infrastructure does not grow apace, the stormwater may combine with sewage flows and, instead of routing to sewage treatment plants, flow untreated into waterways.

Sustainable stormwater management attempts to mimic the natural environment's conditions prior to building, so as to spread out or eliminate runoff, infiltrating rain and runoff close to where it falls, without taxing the wastewater infrastructure. Sustainable, distributed source-control alternatives that retain or consume pollutants and precipitation include bioretention, biofiltration, surface vegetation, and surface soil organisms.

Effective site design, using low-impact development strategies, seeks to minimize the impervious areas. Impervious areas are built surfaces like pavement and buildings that do not allow water to be absorbed and thus lead to runoff. One way to reduce impervious areas is to cluster buildings together. You can also build a multistory library in order to reduce the library's footprint. The impervious surfaces are also minimized by reducing street widths and the amount of impervious paving. And siting the library near transportation systems can allow you to minimize the size of the parking lot.

Some new technologies can also help. There are now permeable concrete and pavers you can use for parking lots and walkways that allow biofiltration. Healthy soil is also important to an effective way to minimize runoff. Permeable solutions allow stormwater to be absorbed into the Earth, breaking down pollutants through filtration and returning water to its clean, natural state.

Rain gardens and swales are bioretention strategies. Integrated into the landscape, rain gardens allow rainwater runoff from impervious surfaces like roofs, driveways, and parking lots the opportunity to be absorbed. This reduces runoff by allowing stormwater to soak into the ground as opposed to flowing into storm drains and surface waters. Swales are specially constructed depressions that can absorb runoff and, if constructed properly, can also enhance the visual landscaping.

Trees, although they need water, are also an essential part of the urban infrastructure and promote carbon sequestration and stormwater management. Trees have the ability to take in, hold, filter, and slowly release large volumes of water. Trees can be a cost-effective way to improve water quality, which is why their preservation and replacement are a fundamental strategy of low-impact development. Besides their role in preserving or improving water quality and stormwater management, trees provide other important functions such as privacy, noise control, temperature buffering, glare reduction, particulate filtering, erosion control, wind control, and, of course, aesthetic beauty. It is no wonder that cities have adopted urban forestation plans. If your city has one, learn about it and become a part of it.

Not all the stormwater management need to take place on the ground. No matter how large the building's footprint, the roof above is comparable in size and can be part of the solution. A green roof is a vegetated space on top of a building. Green roofs provide a variety of benefits including stormwater management, more habitat, longer roof life, and reduced cooling loads within. Depending upon the roof pitch and the building's structural capacity, a green roof can have a variety of soil depths that will dictate the types of plants that can be used.

Xeriscaping

Xeriscaping refers to landscaping that uses very little water for its maintenance. Sometimes called dry landscaping, it uses design elements, plant choices, and best practices like mulching to keep water use to a minimum.

Xeriscaping can help you save water and money and it will also result in landscape that blends with the surrounding area.[12] If done correctly, the xeriscape will use minimum water after the plants are established, will need no herbicides, will use water efficiently and prevent runoff, and will encourage wildlife habitat. Plants, well chosen, should need very little water after a few years.

You can xeriscape a garden on the ground or on the vertical. A vertical garden is often called a living or green wall. Living walls are self-sufficient vertical gardens that are attached to the exterior or interior of a building. They differ from green façades (e.g., ivy walls) in that the plants root in a structural support that is fastened to the wall itself. The plants receive water and nutrients from within the vertical support instead of from the ground. Using the appropriate plant material, these walls can provide many and varied benefits depending on whether they are installed indoors or out. In locations where code allows greywater to be used to water the plants, it can be purified by percolating through the wall. With a long enough passage, the water can be reused as utility water.

Turf

When deciding on what plant material or trees to plant where, consider just how much turf (grass) is necessary to your landscaping scheme. Traditional turf has a high water requirement when compared to other groundcovers and ornamental plants. To keep it green it also needs fertilizer. Many fertilizers are quick-release, containing nitrogen and phosphorous that will pollute the watersheds. Herbicides and pesticides that are applied negatively affect non-targeted plants and wildlife, make their way into the food chain, and compromise air quality, both inside and out. Finally, turf maintenance equipment is usually gasoline-powered with no emission controls and thereby contributes high ratios of carbon dioxide to the greenhouse effect. It is appropriate to decide what turf is necessary and why. Is there a functional reason for the turf such as need for a surface for playing? If not, choose a groundcover that doesn't need mowing, much water or fertilizer and will look pleasing to the eye.

Irrigation Systems

If you need irrigation, consider a drip irrigation system that delivers water at low volumes specifically to plant root zones. Drip systems can be above ground or shallowly buried in soil or decorative rock.

There is also a variety of sensing irrigation equipment to use with more traditional systems that might be already installed or needed for the small patches of turf. Rain-shutoff valves, flow sensors, and check valves can lower water use. You might also be able to install irrigation (or deduct) meters. These meters are used to measure the amount of water used for irrigation that soaks into the earth and does not enter the municipal wastewater system.

Finally, it is important to audit the irrigation system after installation or upgrade, using audit precipitation rates to set controller run times. Be sure a commissioning agent verifies that the system was installed properly and operating efficiently. Library facilities staff needs to know how to audit the irrigation system and use the results to adjust the system appropriately.

Rainwater Harvesting and Downspout Disconnecting

Rainwater harvesting systems collect and store rainfall for later use. Rainwater harvesting systems slow and reduce runoff and provide a source of water. These systems have become particularly attractive in arid regions, where they reduce demands on increasingly limited water supplies. Rainwater for irrigation and other outdoor water uses can be collected in cisterns or rain barrels. Commercial rooftop systems with greater capacity are also available. Yet simply diverting your downspout into a covered rain barrel is an easy, low-cost approach, especially if the amount needed for outdoor uses is minimal. Be aware that some states' water resource agencies do not allow rainwater collection. These prohibitions, however, are disappearing, as rainwater systems become more popular. The library could install such a system that could be used as a community demonstration project.

On-Site Water Treatment

When you think of on-site water treatment, you likely think of septic tanks. Over the last half century, cities have done what they can to eliminate the use of septic systems and add buildings within the city to a city wastewater system. In fact, it has been determined that due to geological and hydrological conditions, two-thirds of the United States is unsuitable for septic systems. Costly system failures and the release of pollutants may result if a septic system is improperly sited. Rather than figure out better on-site systems, "developed countries have transformed fears about these very real sanitation concerns into complex and counterproductive phobias." Municipalities have constructed "incredibly elaborate, energy-intensive systems that not only allow us ready access to potable water from our taps but also insist that we use this most precious resource to flush our toilets." In our desire for water purity, we have "substantially degraded our fresh water supplies."[13]

According to the International Living Futures Organization, "Our water infrastructure, flawed at the best of times, is now on the brink of collapse."[14] The United States alone is faced with spending $330 billion over the next two decades simply to keep our existing tap water systems functioning.[15]

Fortunately, many alternative decentralized wastewater technologies have been developed for situations where conventional systems are not appropriate. These same systems are beginning to be considered for more general use.

If properly designed, installed, and executed, they can protect public health, preserve valuable water resources, and maintain economic vitality in a community. EPA concluded that "adequately managed decentralized wastewater systems are a cost-effective and long-term option for meeting public health and water quality goals, particularly in less densely populated areas."[16] One such system that has been given much attention is the Living Machine. [17] It is for wastewater treatment and has a series of components through which the wastewater flows. The components included in this Living Machine are a clarifier, a subsurface flow wetland, biological treatment reactors, and ultraviolet disinfection. These systems take care of wastewater from a single building or a cluster of buildings.

Water Budgeting Approach

Ask your landscape designer to use a water budget approach. A water budget is a site-specific method of calculating an allowable amount of water to be used by the landscape and then designing the landscape to meet this budget. The budget takes into account plant type, plant water needs, irrigation system design, and applied water that the landscape receives either by irrigation or by precipitation based on local climate data. Water budgets must be associated with a specified amount of time, such as a week, month, or year. The calculations are complex and take into account maximum applied water allowance, net evapotranspiration rate, landscape area, plant factor for the zone, and irrigation efficiency. Not the easiest calculation to understand at first blush, there are web tools being developed to assist with the calculations and help interpret the results. One such is the WaterSense Water Budget Tool. [18] This tool was built for landscaping homes, but it would also work for landscaping the property surrounding your library.

COOLING AND HEATING SYSTEMS

Though certainly not the first thing you think of when considering water conservation, you should not forget cooling and heating systems. If you were to install a water-cooled system, a boiler, or a cooling tower, look at the way water is used in the system. Avoid single-pass systems, where water runs through the system only once before being discharged as wastewater. Instead use close-loop systems.

COMMISSIONING AND AUDITS

Despite the best intentions, actual use sometimes does not match your design. For that reason, it is best to commission the water systems before move in and audit water use on an ongoing basis. Commissioning, addressed in chapter 8, "Building Operations and Maintenance," is the process by which the equipment or system or facility is tested to verify if it functions according to design specifications and objectives.[19]

You should audit your water systems on an ongoing basis. Many jurisdictions have water programs that provide in-house or contracted commercial water audit services. Or you might have someone in your facilities department who could do the auditing. However it occurs, there are several steps involved:

1. Review your library's utility bills for potential leaks. (Use established numbers that are either from the commissioning or immediately following, when there are no leaks, as your baseline numbers. Any numbers out of the ordinary might indicate that leaks have developed.)
2. Read your library's water meter.
3. Systematically monitor high-water-use equipment, restrooms, staff room, heating/cooling system, and irrigation system, if supplied by municipal water. Analyze and correct any problems that are identified.

There is an old business management adage that is applicable here: You can't manage what you can't measure. Since buildings use about 20 percent of the world's available water, there is plenty of opportunity to use less. Measuring will help you determine how to do so. On average, using water-efficient products and fixtures can reduce water consumption by 15 percent, energy use by 10 percent, and operating costs by 12 percent.[20] Not only does this benefit the environment, but it benefits the library's bottom line.

EXAMPLES

The Surry Hills Library and Community Centre in Sydney, Australia, is a four-story, almost 2,500 square-meter library and community center that includes meeting rooms, a commercial teaching kitchen, and a child care center with an outdoor landscaped play space. It has received several awards, including the 2010 National Award for Sustainable Architecture by the Australian Institute of Architects.

There are many notable features about this library, including a unique, environmental atrium and air quality system using the natural filtering properties of plants. Air is naturally cooled under the building, reducing the need for artificial cooling by some 50 percent. Reading about every aspect of this building is interesting and informative, but the features related to this chapter are those related to water conservation.

Rainwater is collected, treated, and reused for the flushing of toilets and irrigation and for watering the atrium plants and lawn. A subterranean tank that stores the rainwater is concealed by a green space. The use of rainwater saves over 620,000 liters of water per year. A green roof is atop the building. All tap fixtures are touch-sensitive and plant equipment will be air-cooled, not water-cooled.[21]

A second example of water conservation is the award-winning xeriscape garden at the Glendale Public Library in Glendale, Arizona. The garden contains over 400 species of desert-adapted native and non-native plants. Signs identify many of the plants, and there is a free audio tour available. This garden is an example of saving water and providing the community with an educational opportunity at the same time.[22]

A third library example is the Green Hills Public Library in Palos Hills, Illinois. After removing a traditional parking lot, a rainwater catchment system was installed and permeable pavers replaced the original pavement. Rainwater from the catchment system gets funneled into the reservoir and then pumped to a small decorative feature and a drip irrigation system for the property. The Green Hills Public Library uses the rainwater harvesting system as an education tool.[23]

Although not a library example, Clatsop Community College has installed a Living Machine, an innovative wastewater system that serves three campus buildings. The website illustrating the machine is worth reviewing if a living system is something you are considering.[24]

YOUR PROJECT NOTES

1. Review the questions posed in the Overview of Sustainable Water Approaches section of this chapter. What are your thoughts? How can you apply your conclusions about these approaches to your project as you answer the more detailed questions that follow?

2. In what climatic region do you live? What are the sources and uses of water in your city or region? What conservation efforts are already under way? How can your library join those efforts? What best practices can your library adopt to secure its water supply?

3. How much of the natural vegetation can you preserve? What vegetation can you plant that is native to your area?

4. Is rain harvesting something that is possible in your area? If so, can you library incorporate it into its design?

5. Is a green roof something that makes sense for your library project?

6. What fixtures and faucets do you need? After doing your research, what fixtures will your library use and how will they conserve water?

NOTES

1. "Water: The Power, Promise and Turmoil of America's Fresh Water," *National Geographic* 184, no. 5A (1993).

2. *Science of Everyday Things*, Hydrological Cycle, Gale, http://www.answers.com/topic/hydrology.

3. Gardner-Outlaw and Engleman, 1997; UNFPA, 1997; "Vital Water Graphics: An Overview of the State of the World's Fresh and Marine Waters—2nd edition," 2008, http://www.unep.org/dewa/vitalwater/article141.html.

4. "U.S. Water Shortages Loom," *Homeland Security News Wire*, February 24, 2012, http://www.homelandsecuritynewswire.com/dr20120224-u-s-water-shortages-loom.

5. World Health Organization, "Water Sanitation Health," http://www.who.int/water_sanitation_health/facts_figures/en/index.html.

6. Clay J. Landry and Terry L. Anderson, "The Rising Tide of Water Markets," WestWater Research, http://www.waterexchange.com/UserFiles/File/dataroom/RisingTideofWaterMarketsbyLandryandAnderson.pdf.

7. Consortium for Energy Efficiency, "CEE Commercial Kitchens Initiative Program Guidance on Pre-Rinse Spray Valves," http://www.docstoc.com/docs/22135671/CEE-Commercial-Kitchens-Initiative-Program-Guidance-on-Pre-Rinse-Spray.

8. EPA, "Energy Star: Clothes Washer," http://www.energystar.gov/index.cfm?fuseaction=find_a_product.showProductGroup&pgw_code=CW.

9. EPA, "Indoor Water Use in the United States," http://www.epa.gov/WaterSense/pubs/indoor.html.

10. Alliance for Water Efficiency, "Maximum Performance (MaP) Testing," http://www.allianceforwaterefficiency.org/Maximum_Performance_(MaP)_Testing.aspx.

11. EPA, "WaterSense: Urinals," http://www.epa.gov/WaterSense/products/urinals.html.

12. Marie Iannotti, "Xeriscape Gardening—Planning for a Water Wise Garden: Simple Steps to a Xeriscaped Garden," About.com Guide, http://gardening.about.com/od/gardendesign/a/Xeriscaping_2.htm.

13. International Living Future Organization, "Water," http://www.living-future.org/node/62.

14. "Water," International Living Future Organization.

15. Charles Duhigg, "Toxic Waters: Saving U.S. Water and Sewer Systems Would Be Costly," *New York Times*, March 15, 2010, http://www.nytimes.com/2010/03/15/us/15water.html?scp=3&sq=water&st=cse.

16. EPA, "Septic (Onsite/Decentralized) Systems," http://water.epa.gov/infrastructure/septic/index.cfm.

17. Living Machine, http://www.livingmachines.com/About-Living-Machine.aspx.

18. EPA, "WaterSense: Water Budget Tool," http://epa.gov/watersense/water_budget/.

19. BusinessDictionary.com, http://www.businessdictionary.com/.

20. "10 Tips for Making Your Building Work," Johnson Controls, http://www.makeyourbuildingswork.com/efficiency-tips/conserve-water/.

21. Bridgette Meinhold, "Australia's Surry Hills Library Sets New Standard for Green Design," *Inhabitat*, http://inhabitat.com/surry-hills-library-australias-new-standard-of-sustainable-excellence/.

22. Glendale Public Library, "Home Page of the Glendale Xeriscape Botanical Garden," http://web.gccaz.edu/glendalelibrary/.

23. Marissa Heflin, "Education Popularizes Rainwater Harvesting," WaterGardenNews.com, 2012, http://www.watergardennews.com/web-exclusives/education-popularizes-rainwater-harvesting.aspx.

24. Clatsop Community College, https://www.clatsopcc.edu/about-ccc/campuses/merts/living-machine.

RESOURCES

Alliance for Water Efficiency. http://allianceforwaterefficiency.org/. The Alliance for Water Efficiency is a stakeholder-based 501(c)(3) non-profit organization dedicated to the efficient and sustainable use of water. The site includes an online resource library.

American Society of Landscape Architects. http://asla.org/. Founded in 1899, the society has twelve thousand members. The site includes a buyers' guide on landscape information.

ARCSA: The American Rainwater Catchment Systems Association. http://www.arcsa.org/. ARCSA consists of professionals working in city, state, and federal government, academia, manufacturers and suppliers of rainwater harvesting equipment, consultants, and other interested individuals.

Ask Nature. http://www.asknature.org/. A free, open source project, built by the community and for the community. The goal is to connect innovative minds with life's best ideas and, in the process, inspire technologies that create conditions conducive to life. To accomplish this, the project includes the organization of the world's biological literature by function.

The Biomimicry Institute. http://biomimicry.net/. The Biomimicry Institute promotes learning from and then emulating natural forms, processes, and ecosystems to create more sustainable and healthier human technologies and designs.

Castle, Anne J. "Water Rights Law: Prior Appropriation." FindLaw for Legal Professionals. 2008. http://corporate.findlaw.com/business-operations/water-rights-law-prior-appropriation.html.

Center for Irrigation Technology, California State University, Fresno. http://cit.cati.csufresno.edu/. An independent research and testing facility, the Center for Irrigation Technology (CIT) plays a vital role in assisting designers, manufacturers, and users of irrigation equipment to make the technological advances required for our growing, changing world.

Environmental Protection Agency. "Case Studies of Sustainable Water and Wastewater Pricing." http://www.epa.gov/safewater/smallsystems/pdfs/guide_smallsystems_fullcost_pricing_case_studies.pdf. Sustainable water pricing seeks to price water with its true value as an increasingly scarce resource.

Environmental Protection Agency. "Climate Change: Human Health Impacts and Adaptation." http://www.epa.gov/climatechange/impacts-adaptation/health.html. Climate change is happening. Even small changes in the average temperature of the planet can translate to large and potentially dangerous shifts in climate and weather. This site discusses what is happening and how to mitigate it.

Environmental Protection Agency. "Water Infrastructure." http://water.epa.gov/infrastructure/. A wealth of information including information reported by the states to EPA about the conditions in their surface waters. Available by zip code.

Environmental Protection Agency. "What Is Nonpoint Source Pollution?" http://water.epa.gov/polwaste/nps/whatis.cfm. Information about nonpoint source pollution which generally results from land runoff, precipitation, atmospheric deposition, drainage, seepage, or hydrologic modification.

Flow: For Love of Water. Directed by Irena Salnia (2008). Award-winning documentary investigation into what experts label the most important political and environmental issue of the twenty-first century: the world water crisis.

Green Roofs for Healthy Cities. http://www.greenroofs.org/. A rapidly growing, not-for-profit, industry association working to promote the industry throughout North America.

Grid Arendal, UNEP. http://www.grida.no/. Environmental Knowledge for Change.

"Growing Healthy Soil: The Natural Lawn and Garden Healthy Landscapes for a Healthy Environment." http://www.seattle.gov/util/groups/public/@spu/@conservation/documents/webcontent/growinghe_200311261701557.pdf. Improving your soil can help you beautify your garden, cut your water bill, improve the water quality in our streams, and even reduce your work.

Intergovernmental Panel on Climate Change. http://www.ipcc.ch/. The Intergovernmental Panel on Climate Change (IPCC) is the leading international body for the assessment of climate change. Be sure to look at the IPCC Fourth Assessment Report: Climate Change 2007, chapter 3, "Freshwater Resources and Their Management."

"Map: Water Basins of North America Map." waterwiki.net. http://waterwiki.net/index.php/Map:_Water_Basins_of_North_America.

National Resources Defense Council. http://www.nrdc.org/. NRDC is a national environmental action group.

Nature Conservancy. http://www.nature.org/. Working with you to make a positive impact around the world in more than 30 countries, all 50 states, and your backyard.

Society for Ecological Restoration (SER). http://www.ser.org/. SER is dedicated to reversing this degradation and restoring the Earth's ecological balance for the benefit of humans and nature.

Stormwater Manager's Resource Center (SMRC). http://www.stormwatercenter.net/. SMRC is designed specifically for stormwater practitioners, local government officials, and others that need technical assistance on stormwater management issues.

Sustainable Sites Initiative. http://www.sustainablesites.org/about/. The Sustainable Sites Initiative (SITES) was created to promote sustainable land development and management practices that can apply to sites with and without buildings.

U.S. Geological Survey. "Estimated Use of Water in the United States." http://water.usgs.gov/watuse/. Data compilation regarding water use in the United States. Scheduled every five years, but compilations may be delayed.

"Water: Doing More with Less." *Environmental Building News*. http://www.buildinggreen. com/auth/article.cfm/2008/2/3/Water-Doing-More-With-Less/. This article looks at strategies for reducing water use in and around buildings, addressing both residential and commercial water uses.

WaterSense, EPA http://www.epa.gov/watersense/faq.html. WaterSense is an EPA program that partners with manufacturers, retailers and distributors, and utilities to bring WaterSense-labeled products to the marketplace and make it easy to purchase high-performing, water-efficient products. WaterSense also partners with irrigation professionals and irrigation certification programs to promote water-efficient landscape irrigation practices.

WaterWiser: The Water Efficiency Clearinghouse. http://www.awwa.org/Resources/ Waterwiser.cfm?navItemNumber=1516. The goal of WaterWiser is to be the premier water conservation, efficiency, and demand management information resource. WaterWiser is an interactive website that strives to meet the information needs of the water conservation.

Chapter Seven

Construction Management

There's a way to do it better; find it!—Thomas Edison

MANAGING A SUSTAINABLE CONSTRUCTION PROCESS

Thomas Edison had it right. It is important to find a better way. Green building is the better way to construct new libraries or renovate older ones. And the actual construction of the library is another step in the building process, another way to ensure that the building is green and the construction is done with as little impact on the environment and people as possible. Therefore, when thinking about the construction management phase of your library and how it will be done, consider these three questions:

1. What must those responsible for the library construction understand regarding your project?
2. How does the construction process influence the success of sustainable design strategies?
3. What can be done during construction to improve the long-term environmental performance of your library?

What follows will address these questions and give you and your library design team points to consider and decide upon long before the actual construction begins. Included here are three types of plans that need to be developed and suggestions for the contents. These plans need to be in place in order to answer the questions posed above, certainly before construction begins.

CONSTRUCTION DOCUMENTS

The drawings and specifications, otherwise known as the project manual, form a legal and binding document that defines the responsibilities and liabilities of the contractor. For your green library project to be successful, it is imperative that this manual outline in writing all expectations and requirements of the project and that it does so in such a way that communicates well with all the subcontractors involved. If you don't understand the document, likely someone else won't either. The specifications must be precise and thorough. Well-written specifications include roles and responsibilities for all laborers, building materials, floor plans, and payment expectations. Building specifications must comply with electrical and fire codes and account for waste removal and all environmental factors.

There are a number of important things to remember when developing these documents. Someone on the library staff who is familiar with this process and has participated in the design team needs to be in charge of writing the documents. That staff member should be chosen carefully and should be someone thoroughly familiar with construction issues. Once in the draft stages, the document should be reviewed by everyone on the library team with ample time for questions and feedback.

Here are a few general tips to consider when reviewing the draft:

- Be sure to spell out whom the agreement is between. List the name of the construction manager and the property owner or developer and the location of the project. Date the document.
- Indicate the scope of the work to be performed, including all interior and exterior labor and construction, the construction codes that must be followed, and the supervision and coordination required to complete the project.
- Spell out a payment schedule, including information on when requisitions will be due or submitted, establishing for the client a time frame for payment. Be sure to include penalties for work not performed on time or satisfactorily.
- Highlight procedures for change orders or delays in the course of the construction process. All change orders must take into account costs associated with redesign, re-engineering, and material adjustments.
- Summarize the documents by including procedures for default—whether on the part of the owner or contractor—and how claims or disputes will be arbitrated and by whom.
- Include all related drawings and product selections as addenda to the documents. If it isn't part of the construction documents, it isn't binding.
- Construction document templates are available on the web. If you use a template, be sure to use one from a reputable source.

Here are some tips specific to a green project and things of particular concern if your library is to be sustainable:

- First of all, there is no shame in borrowing. No need to reinvent the wheel. If you know of another green library that has been successfully built or renovated recently, particularly a library that is similar to the one you are planning, ask to borrow a copy of their documents as a model. Be sure to ask if there is something that they would have done differently or something they forgot to include in their documents.
- The plan should address any benchmarks or requirements set forth in any green building rating system that you are planning to apply to your library project. Make sure that rating system requirements are included in the General Conditions section and in each applicable section of the construction contract. In particular, pay attention to the specific credits for which the contractor is responsible. That should include any submittal requirements, expectations for meetings, and reporting requirements. Reporting requirements might be one thing that is linked to requests for payment.
- Include more rating system requirements in the document than are needed to meet whatever system threshold you have targeted. If for some reason the contractor does not comply with one or two of the requirements, you do not want to have missed the possibility of winning a particular designation. This is especially true if your state, for instance, requires that you build to a minimum standard. As an example, Washington State requires public buildings over 5,000 square feet to be built, minimally, to LEED® Silver standards. If you include only the minimum necessary to meet Silver, if the contractor fails to comply with one or more of those requirements, your building may lose the certification altogether. If you ask for more than the minimum, if the contractor misses one, you will still have met the overall standard. More to the point, the more credits that you meet, the more sustainable your building, no matter the designation level.
- Also include all product and execution information, including performance specifications that outline only the minimum threshold of green attributes required. For instance, be sure to specify information such as recycled content, low-emitting, locally sourced, FSC, and other standards as needed to meet your project goals and rating requirements. Also include any testing or verification requirements. It's best to specify product information and requirements rather than specific brands. (See chapter 4, "Green Materials," for a review of green product attributes.)
- Build options into your building plan so that you can adjust your choices according to your budgetary needs. Depending on the item and the area of the building, you may wish to list green building features as an alternative, not to be included in the base price when contractors bid. This is especially useful for features that can be added or subtracted without major rede-

sign, such as solar panels. Once the bid for the base building and alternates are received, the design team can determine what can be included in the project now and what will need to wait for a later phase. Deductive alternatives also work. In this case the "optimum" design is priced and discounts are applied as certain alternatives are removed. If there is a lot of competition in your area, you might consider this approach. It urges contractors to come up with the best price for the green features upfront rather than estimating green features more generally because they fall outside the base price.

SELECTING THE CONTRACTOR

You need to select your contractor early on in order for him or her to be a member of the library's design team. The contractor is key to your library project's success. To help ensure that the library is built correctly, on time, and on budget, the contractor should meet standards set forth by the state in which your library will be built. Include these elements in your selection criteria and documents:

- **Professional licensing:** Many states use professional licensing as a means to regulate activities that are deemed dangerous when performed incorrectly. In most states, construction professionals—including building contractors, electricians, mechanical contractors, and plumbers—are required to have a professional license. A professional license pertains to the individual. There is also an occupational license that pertains to a business.
- **Contractor insurance:** Contractor insurance coverage is important because it helps protect from lawsuits arising from a project. Regardless of whether these lawsuits have merit, all parties named in a suit must spend time and money to refute the claims.
- **Workers' compensation insurance:** Most states require contractors to have workers' compensation insurance. It helps protect the owner, in this case you and the library, from costs that may be passed on to you by an uninsured contractor whose workers are injured as a result of the project. Even though workers' compensation insurance is required by most states, provisions exist that allow exemption from coverage. For example, a state may allow a construction company to exempt some of its corporate officers. These exemptions are generally documented by authorized waivers.
- **General liability insurance:** Whereas workers' compensation insurance covers the cost of an employee's job-related injury or illness, general liability insurance protects against claims from the public that result from

a company's negligent acts or products. General liability insurance generally covers both property damage and bodily injury.

- **Experience:** Libraries are complex buildings. They are often cited, along with hospitals, as some of the more complex facilities to plan and construct. Therefore it is ideal to choose a contractor that has experience building libraries and, better yet, green libraries, or at least other types of green buildings. Check references. You will *live* with your contractor for an extended period of time and with his or her work for many, many years to come. Years ago a fellow librarians said, referring to a long punch list his contractor was ignoring: "My library building hasn't been finished; it has just been abandoned." Better to work with a contractor who manages the project well, ends with a short punch list, and then follows through to address the problems on that list.

- **Integrated design:** As discussed in chapter 1, "The Fundamentals of Sustainable Building," this requires the early formation of a project team, with upfront involvement of the contractor and other key players. This allows the early development of project goals, including the sustainability goals, helping to ensure that these goals are integrated into all aspects of the project and their successful completion. Depending upon your agency's contracting processes you may want to consider using a contracting method like integrated project delivery (IPD). IPD is a formal contractual structure between owner, contractor, and architect that was developed by the American Institute of Architects.[1] One way or the other, it is important to develop a scope of work that includes contractor participation in an integrated design process, materials research, and costing of concepts and alternatives. Finally, when considering the design, the contractor and design team should take into consideration the library's eventual deconstruction. Both concepts are discussed in chapter 4, "Green Materials."

CONSTRUCTION DEBRIS MANAGEMENT

EPA estimated that 136 million tons of building-related construction and demolition (C&D) materials were generated in the United States in 1996. Most comes from demolition and renovation and the rest from new construction. In addition, the EPA notes:

- Roughly equal percentages of building-related waste are estimated to come from the residential and commercial building sectors.
- The estimated per capita generation rate for building-related debris in 1996 was 2.8 pounds per person per day.[2]

Many residual materials leaving a construction site are recyclable, but the actual percentage that is reused or recycled is dependent on both project management and local infrastructure. The library project design team must plan to eliminate waste where possible, minimize waste where feasible, and reuse or donate materials that might otherwise become waste. In addition, the local area must have the capacity to recycle the concrete, wood, metal, and other materials that come from the job site. What is left must be disposed of responsibly either in a landfill or at a waste-to-energy facility.

CONSTRUCTION WASTE MANAGEMENT PLAN (CWMP)

Whether or not your local jurisdiction or your green building standard requires a construction waste management plan, you will want to have one. Ask your contractor to develop and implement a CWMP consisting of waste identification, waste reduction work plan, and cost/revenue analysis. Include separate sections in plan for demolition and construction waste. All of these elements should be included in a larger section focused on environmental protection. Other elements of the plan should include logistics, any drawings, traffic studies, and emergency measures. The plan should indicate quantities by weight or volume using the same units of measure throughout the CWMP.

Based on research and analysis, develop the plan to include goals (what percentage of debris will be diverted by weight or by volume?); project debris analysis (what will be generated and how much?); materials handling procedures (how will the debris be handled?); communication (how will you tell the construction workers about the plan and be sure that there is participation?); reporting (how will you track it and share results?); and what requirements regarding recycling need to be met if you are using a rating system.

There are many ways to reduce project waste. For instance, use reusable form work, pre-cast concrete, panelized construction, advanced framing, as well as other products and techniques. It is also important to be deliberate in the ways materials are purchased and handled. It is important to prevent the damage of materials from weather or accident. Purchase materials in reduced packaging, even if you have to ask vendors to reduce the packaging. The contractor can also order pre-cut pieces to avoid sizing waste. Also, the contractor should set up just-in-time delivery to reduce storage and potential on-site damage. Recycle, donate, or otherwise divert whenever possible. There are many strategies to reduce waste, including grinding asphalt for use as backfill. In the case of renovated buildings, wood from the initial structures might find its way into the renovation in the form of countertops or furniture.

Hazardous Waste Disposal

Proper storage and disposal of construction materials and hazardous wastes from the construction site prevents the discharge of pollutants into storm water, storm drains, and watercourses. Managing hazardous wastes—to reduce potential risks to project personnel and the site—requires knowledge and diligence on the part of the contractor and the entire design team. Hazardous waste might include spills or leaks of construction materials such as concrete curing compounds, asphalt products, paints, petroleum products from equipment operation and maintenance, septic wastes, pesticides and herbicides, or any material deemed hazardous by the applicable governmental jurisdictions. It is important to become informed of the regulations governing hazardous material well in advance. Try to avoid their use if at all possible, thus reducing the efforts needed to manage them. However, when renovating, it is not always possible to avoid hazardous wastes, since some, such as lead-based paints and asbestos, might be present in the current structure.

Optimize the Use of Recycling

Embedded energy in materials has an environmental cost. Recycling the materials conserves energy and protects the environment. Thus, recycling is an important part of your construction management plan. The first step in planning for recycling is to find out what recycling services are available in your area. What can be recycled? What method of recycling is used? Source-separated or commingled? These factors will determine how the recycling is set up on the construction site. Where are the recycling bins located? Are they as close as possible to where the recycling is generated? It is easy to access by the hauler? Will you need separate bins because the recycling needs to be sorted at the site? Can all the materials be placed in a single container, as is possible with commingled recycling? As you consider the services available), consider too these elements:

- Kinds of materials that will be recycled
- Recycling rate
- Container cost and frequency of pick-up
- Space required
- Garbage disposal
- Documentation required

You also need to evaluate how cost-effective recycling might be for your library. This is largely related to the tipping fees in your area. However there are also other costs to consider when doing your analysis of recycling:

- Container rental costs
- Hauling fees
- Labor
- Documentation
- Taxes

The contractor should submit to you, the owner, as well as the architect, a draft CWMP. Once the owner and architect have determined that the draft plan is acceptable, the contractor can finalize the plan and submit it accordingly. Since you are familiar with the plan, you as well as the architect and others on the design team can monitor the site being sure that the plan is followed.

SOIL AND WATER MANAGEMENT PLAN

Soil is an important element of our urban infrastructure. It is especially important in regulating stormwater runoff and in supporting trees, shrubs, lawns, and gardens. Soil erosion during construction is often a serious problem. Many erosion control practices are available in local soil and water conservation district offices.

Erosion from construction sites causes both on-site and off-site damages. Preventing soil-related problems before they occur is easier and more cost-effective than correcting them later. The library design team needs to be sure that site protection is a part of the construction management plan, and that the contractor and others adhere to both local regulation and best practice.

Here are some best practices regarding erosion control on construction sites. They are adapted from Brady and Weil[3] and first appeared in *Soil Quality—Urban Technical Note, No.1* (USDA/NRCS):

1. Divide the project into smaller phases, clearing smaller areas of vegetation.
2. Schedule excavation during low-rainfall periods, when possible.
3. Fit development to the terrain.
4. Excavate immediately before construction instead of leaving soils exposed for months or years.
5. Cover disturbed soils as soon as possible with vegetation or other materials (mulch) to reduce erosion potential.
6. Divert water from disturbed areas.
7. Control concentrated flow and runoff to reduce the volume and velocity of water from work sites to prevent formation of rills and gullies.
8. Minimize length and steepness of slopes (e.g., use bench terraces).
9. Prevent sediment movement off-site.

10. Inspect and maintain any structural control measures.
11. Where wind erosion is a concern, plan and install windbreaks.
12. Avoid soil compaction by restricting the use of trucks and heavy equipment to limited areas.
13. Soils compacted by grading need to be broken up or tilled prior to vegetating or placing sod.[4]

These best practices should become part of a soil and water management plan. It is the contractor's responsibility to develop this plan in accordance with all relevant regional codes and requirements. As above, the design team members will want to review the draft plan before it is finalized. Then, as the librarian and design team member, it is best to monitor the site and make sure the plan is being implemented.

CONSTRUCTION INDOOR AIR QUALITY (IAQ) MANAGEMENT PLAN

Building construction inevitably introduces contaminates into the library. If not addressed, the contamination can result in poor indoor air quality extending over the lifetime of the building. Fortunately there are IAQ management strategies, if instituted during construction and before occupancy, that will minimize potential problems both during and after construction.

Develop a plan to protect library building surfaces, ductwork, and air handling systems during construction and to minimize IAQ problems due to inappropriate construction techniques following SMACNA guidelines.[5] As an example, ductwork should be kept clean and dry with shrink-wrap or Visqueen covers. Filters utilized for temporary ventilation during construction should be changed regularly through the course of construction.

The construction IAQ management plan should be completed before construction begins and should include construction-related IAQ procedures in the pre-construction and construction progress meeting agendas. Education of subcontractors and all field personnel on the goals of the IAQ management plan is essential if the goals are to be met.

Thus construction management for your library project requires three separate plans. In every plan it is important to incorporate any benchmarks or requirements set forth in any green building rating system that you are planning to apply to your project. For example, LEED has requirements for the minimum MERV ratings on filters used both during construction and after occupancy. MERV filter ratings for during construction would need to be called out in the plan if you were pursuing LEED. Likewise, there are specific requirements to meet recycling credits in LEED and these too would need to be factored in.

EXAMPLES

According to the Forish Construction website, Forish Construction constructed the Pearle L. Crawford Library in Dudley, Massachusetts, as a one-
level library building in a way that would allow the library to "grow with
their community." The design incorporates many green features.

When it came to the construction, the company was responsible in keeping this project LEED certified from the demolition and removal to the
finished building. Forish Construction's activities that led to LEED certification credits, among many others:

- Construction activity pollution prevention
- Construction waste management
- Construction indoor air quality management

All of these elements were discussed in this chapter. Other credits will keep
this building green for the future:

- Light pollution reduction
- Water efficient landscaping
- Water use reduction
- Optimize energy performance
- On-site renewable energy (photovoltaic solar panels)
- Low-emitting materials (all materials used on the job include adhesives,
  sealants, paints, and carpeting below the VOC limits allowed by LEED)
- LEED-accredited professionals[6]

Griffin Structures served as program and construction manager for the
renovation and new construction of the Fullerton Main Library in Fullerton,
California. According to Griffin Structures, the project consisted of a renovation of approximately 30,000 square feet and an addition of approximately
8,000 square feet, designed and constructed to LEED Gold standards.

According to Maureen Gebelein, library director, "Griffin Structures, program and construction manager for the City of Fullerton, served as a strong
partner as the project progressed and continued to be involved with the
Fullerton community. Hard Hat Tours and receptions for community mem-
bers/donors were arranged and Griffin was always there to help us explain
the project to the public and potential donors. Griffin has been exceptionally
cooperative and collegial to work with, and they have really listened to our
needs. We had some specific phasing ideas that would allow us to keep the
library open for as long as possible and they worked to make that happen.
They have been creative in housing construction offices in the library, which

maximizes the dollars going directly into the project rather than temporary construction offices."

The remodel and expansion of the Fullerton Public Library is comprised of a large community meeting room, kitchen, café, and bookstore; an expanded local history area, a new teen services area, and a technology center were remodeled from the existing facilities. In addition, the finish materials, lighting, and furnishings were also enhanced throughout the facility. The exterior renovation, including additional windows, new materials, and landscape, works together with the expansion to provide the building with a fresh and progressive image.[7]

YOUR PROJECT NOTES

1. Revisit the site if possible to review the draft plans. Have you taken all the elements of the site into consideration?

2. What time of year are you building or renovating your library? How soon will your HVAC system be installed? Will you need it to dry out materials? The more the HVAC is used, the more chance to disturb and distribute particulates. How might this be prevented or at least mitigated, given the layout of the building?

3. When should you start the plans addressed in this chapter? Even though the contractor is responsible, it is best for your library design team to develop a list of things specific to your site, your building, and your project that will need to be included in the construction, indoor air quality, and soil management plans?

4. As suggested in the Fullerton Public Library example, it is possible to use the construction phase of your project for fundraising and education. What

possibilities can you imagine? Talk these possibilities over with potential contractors.

NOTES

1. AIA, "Integrated Project Delivery: A Guide," http://www.aia.org/contractdocs/AIAS077630.
2. EPA, "Waste—Non-Hazardous Waste—Industrial Waste," http://www.epa.gov/osw/nonhaz/industrial/cd/basic.htm.
3. N. C. Brady and R. P. Weil, eds., *The Nature and Properties of Soils* (Upper Saddle River, NJ: Prentice Hall, 1999). In 2002 a newer edition was published.
4. U.S. Department of Agriculture, National Resources Conservation Services, "Soil Quality—Urban Technical Note, No. 1," http://infohouse.p2ric.org/ref/02/01524/Urban_Technical_Note_1.htm.
5. SMACNA: Sheet Metal and Air Conditioning Contractors' National Association, http://www.smacna.org/.
6. Forish Construction Company, http://www.forishconstruction.com/Dudley_Library_Project.
7. Griffin Structures, http://www.griffinholdings.net/structures/portfolio/fullerton-library-renovation-expansion-leed-gold.

RESOURCES

American Institute of Architects (AIA), AIA National/AIA California Council. "Integrated Project Management, Version 1." http://www.aia.org/groups/aia/documents/pdf/aiab083423.pdf. This approach integrates people, systems, business structures, and practices into a process that collaboratively harnesses the talents and insights of all the participants to optimize project results, increase value to the owner, reduce waste, and maximize efficiency through all phases of the project.
Environmental Protection Agency. "Greening EPA: Waste Diversion." http://www.epa.gov/oaintrnt/waste/index.htm. EPA's most recent information regarding waste diversion.
Environmental Protection Agency. "Stormwater Management Best Practices." http://www.epa.gov/oaintrnt/stormwater/best_practices.htm. EPA facilities draw on best practices, also called integrated management practices (IMPs), to design, implement, and evaluate their stormwater management efforts.
Napier, Tom. *Construction Waste Management*. Whole Building Design Guide, March 6, 2012. http://www.wbdg.org/resources/cwmgmt.php. Solid waste management practices have identified the reduction, recycling, and reuse of wastes as essential for sustainable management of resources.
Reckson, A Division of SL Green. "Construction IAQ Management Plan." December 1, 2011. http://slgreen.com/reckson/pdf/IAQ-Construction-Rules-Regs.pdf. A sample.

Chapter Eight

Building Operations and Maintenance

*You never change things by fighting the existing reality. To change something,
build a new model that makes the existing model obsolete.*—B. Fuller

THE NEED FOR COMMISSIONING AND BUILDING
OPERATIONS AND MAINTENANCE

Buckminster Fuller probably wasn't thinking about buildings operations and
maintenance when he said the quote above, but his comments are apt. In
order to get the most out of your green library and to make a positive difference on the environment and the library's bottom line, commissioning and
facilities management must be green propositions. Both are necessary to
assure that the green building that you just built or renovated is green and
stays green.

Commissioning (Cx) begins at project design and ends either when the
library construction is complete or a year beyond that date; facilities management begins when the library is turned over to the library working efficiently.
Long-term stewardship of the library requires that the facilities manager and
the staff have the skills, desire, and commitment to engage in sustainable
building practices. However, as is often the case, facilities management does
not get the attention or the funding required to ensure that the library is
efficient and productive for staff and an inviting, engaging, healthy learning
space for the people you serve. Within the past decade, commissioning has
received more attention because it is a requirement of green standards such
as LEED®.

BUILDING COMMISSIONING

According to the Building Commissioning Association, building commissioning "provides documented confirmation that building systems function according to criteria set forth in the project documents to satisfy the owner's operational needs. Commissioning existing systems may require developing new functional criteria to address the owner's current requirements for system performance."[1] The systems to be commissioned will vary from project to project but will likely include HVAC, plumbing, electrical, lighting, fire/life safety, building envelope, wastewater, controls, and building security.

Commissioning is often thought to focus solely on testing during the end of the construction phase. However, commissioning is actually a collaborative process that begins during the planning phase and does not end until the library is operating as intended. ASHRAE (American Society of Heating, Refrigeration and Air-Conditioning Engineers) defines commissioning as "the process of ensuring that systems are designed, installed, functionally tested, and capable of being operated and maintained to perform in conformity with the design intent. . . . Commissioning begins with planning and includes design, construction, start-up, acceptance and training, and can be applied throughout the life of the building." This description depicts commissioning as an integrated process that spans from pre-design planning to post-construction operation to ensure that checks and balances are in place. The steps involved in commissioning are:

1. Define and document requirements clearly at the outset of each phase of the library project and update through the process.
2. Verify and document compliance at each completion level.
3. Establish and document commissioning process tasks for subsequent phases.
4. Deliver buildings and construction projects that meet your (the owner's) needs, at the time of completion.
5. Verify that library operation and maintenance personnel and occupants are properly trained.
6. Maintain facility performance across the library's life cycle.[2]

Commissioning is still a relatively new concept. It is sometimes seen as just an extra hit to the building budget, but it's an important quality assurance strategy. Total building commissioning costs for commissioning agent services can be as low as 0.5 percent of total construction costs. However, the National Association of State Facilities Administrators (NASFA) recommends budgeting 1.25 to 2.25 percent of the total construction costs for commissioning services.[3] There are many factors that will influence commissioning costs, including the extent of the commissioning services needed, the level of commissioning desired, and what systems and assemblies are chosen for commissioning. However, when considering the cost of commissioning systems in your library building, consider total life cycle costs, not simply the library's first costs. Commissioned buildings perform better, with lower recurring costs and better indoor environmental quality.

A 2009 study by Evan Mills responded to end-users who do not have confidence in the nature and level of energy savings that can be achieved through the commissioning process. It is composed of case studies, previously unpublished data, and performance benchmarks using standardized assumptions. Overall, the study reveals that "commissioning is arguably the single-most cost-effective strategy for reducing energy, costs, and greenhouse-gas emissions in buildings today."[4]

Commissioning done as part of renovation and new building projects is completed prior to occupancy. Enhanced commissioning is a set of best practices that go beyond fundamental commissioning to ensure that building systems perform as intended by the owner. These practices include designating a commissioning authority prior to the construction documents phase, conducting commissioning design reviews, reviewing contractor submittals, developing a systems manual, verifying operator training, and performing a post-occupancy operations review generally within a year after the building's substantial completion. In the case of LEED 2009, there are several additional steps involved in enhanced commissioning, including a review of operations and maintenance within ten months of substantial completion, with a plan to resolve outstanding commissioning-related issues.[5]

WHO CAN COMMISSION?

The commissioning agent (CxA) is generally, and preferably, contracted directly to the building owner as a third-party independent representative to ensure unbiased performance. The CxA may be a subcontractor or employee of the building owner (though this is not preferred), architect, design engineer, test and balance contractor, or other trade contractor. The CxA is responsible for the following:

- Assisting with a clear statement of the design intent for each building system in the library
- Writing the commissioning specifications and incorporating them in the appropriate divisions of the construction specifications
- Carrying out pre-functional and functional testing of all equipment and systems to be commissioned, using procedures designed in advance
- Reviewing operations and maintenance (O&M) documents to be provided by the contractor

- Developing operations and maintenance training curricula and materials to ensure they meet needs of operations and maintenance staff
- Writing a final report including all commissioning documentation and recommendations for the owner

If you are using a rating system, be sure to check the rating system's requirements regarding commissioning. These will help guide your process. A rating system will usually call for a third-party verifier, someone hired by the contractor. For instance, the LEED rating system requires that a third-party commissioning agent be engaged for this process.

SUSTAINABLE FACILITY MANAGEMENT (SFM)

The integration of sustainability into the facility management process constitutes a new model of facilities management. However, it is a *natural* fit, so to speak. Facility management professionals have long been concerned with and engaged in the environmental aspects of the facilities they operate, especially from the perspective of energy conservation and high-performance buildings. Over time, facilities management professionals have integrated many other aspects of sustainability.

Today sustainable facility management elements are integrated into custodial services, landscaping practices, transportation, and purchasing. Green techniques and products are constantly being developed, and what follows, therefore, only represents some examples of how to manage your library facility operations.

OPERATIONS AND MAINTENANCE

There are a number of elements to consider when developing your operations and maintenance procedures manual that should be followed by your operations and maintenance staff. Here is an outline of the elements that should be included in the manual:

Custodial Services

- Utilize environmentally friendly products (e.g., Green Seal) and practices.
- Utilize non-paper based hand drying systems.
- Use concentrated cleaning products to reduce the environmental impact on shipping.

Energy and Lighting Performance

- Use the documentation developed during commissioning to monitor and maintain the HVAC systems.
- Turn off all or some of the lights when an area is not in use, particularly when the building is not occupied.
- Keep the fixtures clean so that the light output is not dimmed or blocked.
- Keep windows clean and unobstructed.

Green Landscaping Practices

- Develop and implement a sustainable master landscape plan.
- Utilize a weather-based irrigation system, where irrigation is necessary.
- Utilize reclaimed water for irrigation.
- Implement a green waste-to-mulch program.
- Implement integrated pest management control strategies.

Transportation

- Maintain electric-powered vehicles in your library's carpool, if such exists.
- Recharge your electric-powered vehicles from solar power.

Environmentally Preferred Purchasing (EPP)

- Establish an EPP user group to evaluate products used in facilities maintenance operations for the purpose of using more recycled and environmentally friendly products when economically and operationally feasible.
- Refer to chapters 3 and 4 for information regarding ecofriendly equipment and materials.
- Establish recycling and composting procedures.

Operations and Maintenance Training Program

- Send your operations and maintenance personnel to training. Many such training programs are now available online, either from your local community college or from associations such as the International Facility Management Association or the Building Owners and Managers Association International.
- Establish procedures based on the training.

EXAMPLES

In November 2007, the William J. Clinton Presidential Library, a part of the National Archives, received LEED Platinum certification for existing buildings (LEED-EB) from the U.S. Green Building Council. Efforts to obtain the credit points necessary to achieve Platinum certification required facility manager Steve Samford, LEED AP, to implement several new programs and procedures. These included "efficient use of energy, building commissioning to insure optimum equipment performance, an integrated pest management program, purchasing of environmentally preferred products, waste stream management and ongoing indoor environmental quality." When it opened in 2004, the library complex earned a Silver LEED rating—the first presidential library to do so.[6]

The San Lorenzo Building Expansion Project offers a good example of the request for proposal (rfp) and statement of qualification (soq) for construction management construction services.[7] Of particular note are the specifications for enhanced commissioning (see page 5 and Exhibit Q of the document) and the fact that the enhanced commissioning is included in the scope of services that are being requested from the company who will handle the construction management. This pairing makes good sense for obvious reasons.

In 2011 the West Vancouver Memorial Library became the first existing building in Western Canada, and the only library in Canada, to be awarded LEED for Existing Buildings Silver certification. As part of the certification process the library adopted a green building operations policy. The stated goal of the policy is to guide the library toward "improving building performance, reducing costs, creating more productive and healthy work and public spaces as well as affording the Library the opportunity to take a leadership role in environmental stewardship for our community."[8]

The policy guides plumbing, housekeeping, solid waste management (e.g., recycling and purchasing materials with recycled content), integrated pest management, erosion control, and landscape management. The structure of the policy document is also worth noting. There is a performance metric section that helps define how to "implement, monitor and evaluate sustainable practices."[9]

Having upgraded the controls for the HVAC system, the library is making a concerted effort to manage the power consumption of their 56,000 square feet. They have replaced all single pane windows on one level with automated, energy-efficient windows that are tied to their HVAC system to allow for air cooling. They also use web-based energy management software to track and manage their energy consumption.[10]

The Teton County (Wyoming) Library offers a good example of a very well-developed green operations program.[11] Their program includes energy conservation, electricity conservation, landscaping/water conservation, recycling, and green programs (and workshops). The web page centerpiece is the library's solar panel statistics. As the website states, Teton County Library "works to be a green, sustainable building and operation."

YOUR PROJECT NOTES

1. How large is your library project? If it is major, have you decided on whether you will use commissioning or enhanced commissioning? What would be the ROI for each? Consider a life cycle analysis of the costs and savings.

2. Have you chosen a training program for your operations and maintenance staff? What will need to be in the program? This, of course, is dependent on what systems are in your library and what has been included in your new library building or renovation.

3. Based on the commissioning, what are the performance benchmarks for your systems, such as the HVAC?

4. Are you familiar with EPP programs? Is your agency (e.g., the city, the college) already participating in such a program?

5. How might you model your library's sustainable building operations to your community?

NOTES

1. Building Commissioning Association, https://netforum.avectra.com/eweb/StartPage. aspx?Site=BCA&WebCode=HomePage.

2. *Building Commissioning,* Whole Building Design Guide, http://www.wbdg.org/project/ buildingcomm.php.

3. U.S. General Services Administration, "Commissioning Agent Costs," http://www.gsa. gov/portal/content/101959.

4. "Building Commissioning: A Golden Opportunity for Reducing Energy Costs and Greenhouse-Gas Emissions," http://cx.lbl.gov/2009-assessment.html.

5. *LEED 2009 for New Construction*, U.S. Green Building Council, 2009, 299–303.

6. U.S. National Archives and Records Administration, "Clinton Presidential Library Receives Highest Green Building Rating," November 21, 2007, http://www.archives.gov/press/ press-releases/2008/nr08-28.html. http://www.gsa.gov/portal/content/101959.

7. General Services Agency, County of Alameda, "County of Alameda Construction Management Professional Services Request for Proposal and Statement of Qualifications Specifications, Terms & Conditions for San Lorenzo Library Building Expansion, San Lorenzo, Unincorporated Alameda County Project No. 10034, Networking/ Proposers Conferences," http:// www.acgov.org/gsa/purchasing/bidContent_ftp/rfpDocs/RFP-SOQCM10034.pdf.

8. Rebekkah Smith Aldrich, "Be Inspired by the West Vancouver Memorial Library!" Sustainable Libraries, October 2011, http://sustainablelibraries.org/2011/10/be-inspired-by-the-west-vancouver-memorial-library/.

9. Aldrich, "Be Inspired."

10. Aldrich, "Be Inspired."

11. Teton County Library, "Green Building and Operations," http://tclib.org/index.php/ about_tcl/green/.

RESOURCES

BetterBricks. http://www.betterbricks.com/. BetterBricks champions the guiding principle that commercial buildings should be designed and operated with energy top of mind.

BetterBricks. "Life-Cycle Cost Analysis versus Simple Payback—Why, When, How." BetterBricks. http://www.betterbricks.com/graphics/assets/documents/BB_CostAnalysis_WWW. pdf. Describes when to use simple pay back vs. total cost of ownership calculations.

BOMA: Building Owners and Managers Association. http://www.boma.org/Pages/default. aspx. BOMA International is a primary source of information on building management and operations, development, leasing, building operating costs, energy consumption patterns, local and national building codes, legislation, occupancy statistics, technological developments, and other industry trends.

BOMA. "BOMA 7-Point Challenge," http://www.boma.org/awards/Pages/7-point-challenge.aspx. Started in 2007, the 7-Point Challenge aims to reduce the use of natural resources, nonrenewable energy sources, and waste production and work in coordination with building management, ownership, and tenants to achieve a landmark market transformation. Recently concluded, this website lists the challenges and acknowledges those companies that stepped up to the challenge.

Building Commissioning Association. https://netforum.avectra.com/eweb/Start-Page.aspx?Site=BCA&WebCode=HomePage. The BCA's goal is to achieve high professional standards while allowing for the diverse and creative approaches to building commissioning that benefit our profession and its clients.

Building EQ: Building Energy Quotient: ASHRAE's Building Energy Labeling Program. http://buildingenergyquotient.org/. Control rising energy costs with the Building EQ. Geared to the commercial buildings.

Energy Star. "Purchasing and Procurement." http://www.energystar.gov/index.cfm?c=bulk_purchasing.bus_purchasing. Purchasing efficient products reduces energy costs without compromising quality. Take the steps outlined to learn more about ENERGY STAR qualified products and specify them in your purchasing policies and contracts.

International Facility Management Association. http://ifma.org/. IFMA is the world's largest and most widely recognized international association for facility management professionals.

International Facility Management Association. "Professional Development: Certified Facility Manager (CFM). http://www.ifma.org/professional-development/credentials/certified-facility-manager-cfm. The IFMA offers three credentials. The first two culminate in the Certified Facility Management process, which is designed to assess competence in the field through work experience, education, and the ability to pass a comprehensive exam.

International Facility Management Association. "Sustainability 'How-To' Guide Series." http://www.ifmafoundation.org/research/how-to-guides.htm. The IFMA Foundation, with support from IFMA's Sustainability Committee, is producing a series of white papers to respond to this need for information regarding sustainability and the implementation of energy-saving techniques.

Optimize Operational and Maintenance Practices. Whole Building Design Guide, September 10, 2012. http://www.wbdg.org/design/optimize_om.php. No matter how sustainable a building may have been in its design and construction, it can only remain so if it is operated responsibly and maintained properly. This document explores practices that ensure this occurs.

RPN: Responsible Purchasing Network. http://www.responsiblepurchasing.org/. The RPN is an international network of buyers dedicated to socially responsible and environmentally sustainable purchasing.

U.S. Green Building Council. "LEED for Existing Buildings: Operations and Maintenance." http://www.usgbc.org/ShowFile.aspx?DocumentID=5545. Rating system used to certify an existing building, using sustainable operations and maintenance practices.

Conclusion

If you build it, they will come.—paraphrased from Ray Kinsella, *Shoeless Joe*

IF YOU BUILD IT . . .

If you build or renovate a library, you can expect the world, or at least your community, to be at your door. Although there is lots of anecdotal evidence to bear this out, there is little research on this issue. Perhaps the impact of new facilities on libraries' resources and services is so overwhelming that this assertion is regarded as a truism.

Needless to say, if you have achieved a sense of place befitting your community, it is likely that you will meet or exceed the statistics quoted in a Colorado Library fact sheet.

> When new libraries are built, visits and attendance at library programs increase most dramatically of the three output measures examined. On average, both the number of visits and program attendance for single-outlet libraries increased by more than 35 percent (36 percent for visits, 38 percent for program attendance) from pre- to post-building years, compared to seven percent for both visits and program attendance for all Colorado libraries.
>
> When new libraries are built, more items are checked out. On average, total circulation for single-outlet libraries increased by 16.5 percent for pre- to post-building years, compared to 4.5 percent for all Colorado libraries. [1]

This sort of impact on services and resources will occur whether or not your library is green. You may, in fact, anticipate an even greater impact if your community members have had input into the design process and if you have demonstrated and communicated your library's green values.

129

THE LIBRARY BUILDING AS A TEACHING TOOL

As you design your building, it is important that you consider the ways in which your library building can be an educational tool to teach the community about sustainability and foster behavioral change using similar technologies and techniques at home, at work, and in the community. In fact education is a component of LEED® certification.

There are many ways to promote sustainability. Some sponsor programs related to the green building. Others offer tours. Often the library includes permanent displays in the library to explain the various green features and technologies. The Fayetteville Public Library went beyond these basic techniques to not only improve the sustainability of their operations but also become a community test bed for a renewable energy project.[2] A kiosk in the lobby provides a real-time display of the energy production data from the solar array and provides educational information on solar power.[3] The 2011 solar rebates totaled over $34,000. Those funds were earmarked for other library sustainability initiatives.[4]

LIBRARY RESOURCES

A library may also find other ways to demonstrate its commitment to sustainability. The library can build a collection of materials on sustainability. In this case, the format as well as the content should be considered. Books, periodicals, and digital resources are a given. You might also check out equipment. For instance, the Fayetteville Library participates in the Track and Save program. Track and Save is a new program that will allow library patrons the opportunity to check out kilowatt meters from public libraries throughout Arkansas to measure energy use at home.[5]

EVERYDAY GREEN

As discussed in chapter 8, "Building Operations and Maintenance," routine functions such as operations and maintenance should also be greened. Without making the changes to operations, your library's commitment to sustainability is incomplete. But in its education role, the library can be many small things that collectively make a difference and serve as examples of things that everyone can do. In 2009, Meredith Walker wrote an article entitled "100 Ways to Make Your Library a Little Greener," pointing out that the ways to green day-to-day activities is limited only by one's imagination.[6]

Former director of the award-winning Fayetteville Public Library in Arkansas, Louise Schaper, discussed her library's efforts to align its values and practices in her article "Let 'Green' Creep."[7] "When I looked around at what we were doing, I kept hearing the values that community members clearly articulated during the planning process and could see that we were not carrying them out as we should." She gave some examples:

1. Giving away plastic book bags.
2. Lighting up the sky and using lots of electricity with night cleaning services.
3. Printing thousands of monthly newsletters.
4. Gluing ads for library programs to foam core for display at service desks.
5. Using bottled water and plastic cutlery, cups, and dishes for events.
6. Serving candy and other unhealthy foods at programs.
7. Driving to meetings and restaurants, even if only a few blocks away.
8. Leaving PCs and monitors on 24/7.
9. Adding cooling units and fans to address server and CPU overheating.
10. Offering library cards that couldn't be recycled and wouldn't decompose.

Schaper continued:

> How could we align the green values inherent in the building with operations? With so many of our actions, including mine, I saw activities trending upward in carbon emissions instead of down. What could we do? We were overwhelmed by all the critical things you do when moving into a new building, like tweaking work processes and ensuring that residents get every bit of value for their $23.4 million. Isn't serving a rapidly growing base of customers drawn to a facility that one young adult said was "just like a New York City library" enough? How would we ever have time to make operations greener? Was I sufficiently committed?

By incorporating green principles into not just planning and construction but everyday operations, we can ensure that our libraries contribute to the sustainability of our communities for decades to come.

NOTES

1. Colorado State Library, Colorado Department of Education, "Fast Facts: Recent Statistics from the Library Research Service: Public Use and Support Skyrocket When New Libraries Are Built," ED3/110.10/No. 226, August 22, 2005, http://www.lrs.org/documents/fastfacts/226_public_use.pdf.

2. Fayetteville Public Library, "Green Energy Production Produces Sizeable Rebates," January 19, 2012, http://www.fplsolar.org/.

3. Fayetteville Public Library, "Library to Host Public Project Presentation, Aug. 24," August 19, 2010, http://www.fplsolar.org/.

4. Fayetteville Public Library, "Solar Rebate Approved by Arkansas Energy Office," February 24, 2011, http://www.fplsolar.org/.

5. Fayetteville Public Library, "'Track and Save' Kilowatt Meters Available at the Fayetteville Public Library," April 10, 2012, http://www.faylib.org/news?page=10.

6. http://www.bachelorsdegreeonline.com/blog/2009/100-ways-to-make-your-library-a-little-greener/.

7. Louise Schaper, "Let 'Green' Creep," *Library Journal,* May 29, 2010, http://www.libraryjournal.com/article/CA6727897.html. See also Rebecca Miller's interview with Schaper, "Lead with Green: Q&A with Louise Schaper," *Library Journal*, May 29, 2010, http://lj.libraryjournal.com/2010/05/managing-libraries/lead-with-green-qa-with-louise-schaper/.

Index